'MATCH THE AGE' to 'KEEP THEM ENGAGED'

'MATCH THE AGE' to 'KEEP THEM ENGAGED'

DECODING THE SECRETS OF CREATING A HAPPY WORKPLACE

Deepak Malhotra

BLOOMSBURY

NEW DELHI • LONDON • OXFORD • NEW YORK • SYDNEY

Bloomsbury Publishing India Pvt. Ltd.
DDA Complex LSC, Building No.4
Second Floor, Pocket C-6&7, Vasant Kunj
New Delhi 110070

Bloomsbury is a trademark of Bloomsbury Publishing Plc

ISBN: 978-93-84898-06-9
10 9 8 7 6 5 4 3 2 1

Typeset by Eleven Arts
Printed and bound in India by Thomson Press India Ltd

Acknowledgement

I express my sincere gratitude to my seniors, colleagues, distinguished scholars, friends, and authors, whose works have influenced me over the years in my professional career, research, and training.

I thank my readers, as each individual response was very encouraging; thus, inspiring me to pen my thoughts down in black and white.

My special thanks to my parents, my better half Sayani, and my children Rishi and Diksha for their cooperation at every stage. Sayani needs a specific mention, as she was my first critic, helping me to create stories, and make this book more interesting.

I have always been indebted to the Almighty for his blessings.

I also express my sincere thanks to all the employees of the surveyed organisations, and my fellow human resource professionals for their valuable time and cooperation during the collection of data for my primary research work. I am also grateful to some of my seniors who have shared their valuable insight in the journey. My heartfelt gratitude goes to Bloomsbury Publishing for providing me valuable suggestions and supporting me in the completion of the book.

Dr Deepak Malhotra

Acknowledgement

Contents

Foreword

While we hear incessantly about the potential advantage of the demographic dividend, and the skilling challenges that need to be addressed for this advantage to become a reality, much less attention is paid to what it will mean to manage organisations staffed by this post-millennial workforce.

While the opportunity side has been articulated well by Nandan Nilekani and others who believe that the new generation will be free of the dogmas and limitations of the earlier generations, there are bound to be challenges as well. The new generation, grown up on the mobile and the Internet, is bound to have a shorter attention span, seems to expect frequent appreciation, and thinks all answers are available on Google!

Foreword

At the same time, the human resources function is itself going through many changes. While on the one hand there have been calls to HR managers to engage better with business and for the HR function to become a strategic partner of business, on the other, some organisations have chosen to rely on technology or outsourcing partners to manage the basic HR service functions, and leave day-to-day people management to line managers, thereby practically abdicating the role of HR as we usually understand it.

Fortunately, amidst all this flux, there is a new generation of HR managers who are thoughtful, grounded, and determined to build effective organisations. Deepak Malhotra belongs to this group.

Deepak spends a lot of time with students who are about to graduate, to understand their aspirations and shape their expectations of the workplace. At work, he delegates much of his daily professional activities to his junior colleagues, leaving him time to plan for the future.

In conversation with him, I have found that he has a nuanced view of the people challenges Indian organisations face today, and are likely to confront tomorrow.

I am glad that Deepak has found the time to put his thoughts together in an organised way in the form of this book. I am confident that this timely book will be benefit everyone interested in building robust Indian organisations in the years ahead.

Rishikesha T. Krishnan
Director
Indian Institute of Management Indore (IIM Indore)

X

Foreword

Often, the outcome of the role played by management and human resource leaders is a non-engaged employee. The global current scores of fully engaged employees stand at 13 per cent. Shockingly, the Indian score stands at mere 9 per cent. As a leader, I believe that the reason for non-engagement of employees has to either be that they are not aligned to the leadership and the vision, or are not sufficiently appreciated for their contribution. What are they here for then? Just for salaries? I hate mentally absent and physically present team members.

Through my long career in the corporate world, I have come across the common engagement interventions at an organisation level. Deepak has thought out of the box, and has, looked in detail at the different outlooks of employees which may have been in place, due to generation and attitudinal gaps. When I was younger, my needs were different from current times, and that may apply to most people

I firmly second his thought when I see people around me having different sets of individual needs. The multiple generational mind-sets get exhibited distinctively as below:

- Aspirations, skills, and knowledge gaps
- Technology capabilities
- Self-confidence
- Multi-tasking capabilities
- Ability to seek challenges

Deepak had a very interesting career graph from being a chef in a hotel to a human resource head, and now a writer. He has had a ringside view and has been part of many diverse businesses. His experience with multinationals, as well as domestic and family businesses spread over an array of industries, has provided him with great insights that are evident in the examples he has chosen to illustrate in the book.

Every successful organisation has its distinctive strengths, but also has a common human commitment that works automatically towards building it. Deepak's parable of a casting director makes this book a very interesting read for everyone, especially the way he has appropriately related examples from the corporate world and paralleled them with the film industry.

Deepak has reminded us once again to look for the Indian economic vitality through influencing people by encouraging the entrepreneurial and leadership skills. People leaders play a pivotal role in identifying the right actors with potential, ability, and age, based on organisational needs by 'Matching the Age'. Actors do play the role assigned to them and leaders extract productivity from them by 'Keeping them Engaged'.

Deepak Malhotra's book is positive and innovative as a source of new style of leadership. This material would add to the data, which the Indian management fraternity and business leaders must build on. It is for the first time that someone has penned down his thoughts on one-click generation, Gen Y, Gen X, and elders differently and in such detail. It is tremendous for someone like Deepak to suggest as to how to tackle team members from diverse generations differently, and the ways to keep them engaged. His chapter on current economic scenario and how to keep it going is an eye opener for leaders.

Whatever little I have known of the author, Deepak definitely has lots of stories to share. I have seen him contribute to various B Schools, and his love and passion to contribute for the One- Click Generation is evident. Keeping in mind that India is going to have one of the youngest workforce, I wish Deepak narrates many more such stories to all of us.

I strongly recommend this book to all C-level executives, people leaders, entrepreneurs, academicians, students of all types of management streams (future leaders), and even to people who wish to just engage with others, or parents managing youngsters. Let's just understand that human resources are the responsibility of each and every people leader of every function, and not only of a CEO or an HR head.

By understanding and employing some of the learnings, I am sure you will be in a better position to boost the engagement with your people, and improved productivity and profits would follow automatically.

Sandeep Saxena
Group CEO, Dr Batra's Healthcare

xiii

CHAPTER 1

Abstract

When we, as leaders, study the interface between human needs of varied age groups of employees in an organisation and organisational environment, several significant influencers arise, which affect the employees of the organisation. These factors are related to employees' job satisfaction or dissatisfaction.

The factors could be many, like job content, right tools, accountability, timely recognition by leaders, overall opportunities to learn and grow, overall image of the organisation, company's human resource policies, and other related interventions. In the present world, timely payments, supervision and leadership, interpersonal relationship with subordinates, peers, and superiors, working condition, job safety, independence at work, empowerment, job status and self-esteem, job rotation, learning and development opportunities, etc., have influenced, either by positive or negative impact, the performance of employees.

Post liberalisation, the giant business houses have shown keen interests in investing huge amount of money in the growing sectors like healthcare, hospitality, environment, infrastructure development, ITES, and education. The changing set-up of business is observing a paradigm shift. The growth prospects also have enforced many individual stakeholders to invest in the future.

The key resources of an organisation is its good people, and I have researched extensively on the various motivating influencers for them. I firmly believe that 'happy and engaged people produce better results'.

As a people's manager, you would agree that in every organisation, there is a generation gap, which generates different outlooks. Different age groups differ in skills or knowledge fissures, technology management, self-confidence, multi-tasking drive, and the ability to pursue challenges and work in teams. This is different for different age groups.

2

This initiative is to challenge the traditional one-fit-for-all approach of people leaders, in terms of engagement at an organisational level, and thereby focussing on very basic situational leadership styles, in reference to their teams. This book looks at complete out-of-the-box leadership styles, by 'matching the age' to 'keeping them engaged'. Engagement is defined by some leaders in calendars, activities, or interventions, which is not what engagement is. It is the continuous process of commitment through the right intention by people leaders, to engage their teams, and this zest is the essence of the book.

This is a voyage to study the waves of extrinsic as well as core dynamics of job-satisfaction, entrepreneurial leadership traits, and engagement, which affect the special impetus of employees in different age groups. The book also takes into account the impact of the engagement, and therefore, people management styles, on the overall productivity of organisation, and in turn, on efficiencies and balance sheets.

As 'keeping them engaged' is directly proportionate to productivity, and is one of the major contributors to it, we, as leaders or future leaders reading this book, should be able to realise that organisational success or profits will come only if the teams, whether producing goods or delivering services, are engaged in diverse scenarios. In the current economic situation, it is very challenging but attainable, and that's where our expertise would come into picture.

Then what followed, formed the beginning of the empirical book: 'match the age' to 'keep them engaged'.

3

CHAPTER 2

Introduction

Would you believe when I say most of the workers hate their jobs?

The reason is very simple. As a people's manager, one must realise:

I. Either they are not properly recognised by their superiors.

or

II. They do not feel aligned to the overall company's vision.

They may also feel that they are not contributing to the company's bottom line. In simple words, it means they need encouragement, and they need to be convinced on their role in the organisation.

The next very important question which arises here is, do we need a budget? Well, I don't think so. It simply testifies how positive and effective entrepreneurial leader you are.

The very next question that clicks in our minds is what are they here for? Bang-on! They are just here to receive their remuneration, month after month.

A happy workplace can have significant impact on the business results and the overall success. It is no rocket science to conclude that there is a huge impact of engagement on productivity. The co-relation between engagement and efficiency is proved time and again. The entrepreneurial style of leadership should focus on this relation.

> Just as a casting director engages a particular actor for a role, keeping in mind the story of the movie, the age bracket, and his potential to do justice to the role; a leader similarly plays a pivotal role in identifying the right actors, by 'matching the age', their potential, efficiency, and the dedication to do justice to their assigned jobs. In other words, 'keeping them engaged' and extracting the best out of them.

Many famous studies have been conducted on the subject. Studies of John Helliwell, Emeritus, Martin Seligman (psychologist), D H Myers, J M George, and P. Totterdell indicate that, positive people are those who focus primarily on what is right. These so-called positive people are most often more imaginative, broad-minded, constructive, liberal, and humble in nature. Their listening skills are often better than the rest, and therefore, is the key differentiator in them.

I think most of you would second my thoughts, and the above mentioned skills are what we look at in a leader.

Terminologies like leaders, entrepreneurial leaders or people's leader, or people leaders, would be often used throughout the book for your better understanding. Correct me if I am wrong, an entrepreneurial leader does not always refer to entrepreneurs. It means entrepreneurial style of leadership, which caters to entrepreneurial employees. It is a concept of taking initiative and acting like a business owner, and challenging the status-quo. It is just the mind-set, but it becomes a huge differentiator in the long run. I wanted to clear this at the beginning of the book, as I would refer to this again in the following chapters.

Is the responsibility only with the CEO and the human resource leaders to engage and motivate? I strongly believe in the concept of shop-floor human resources, irrespective of the type of industry. Therefore, engagement and keeping the team happy is also the duty of a people's leader.

This book, therefore, is written for all entrepreneurial, business, and people leaders, future leaders, and academicians, who would handle the coming generations. This book is for everyone, parents and the future parents.

Entrepreneurial leaders are always aware, boosting performance through enabling environment, work-life balance, tangible rewards, and communication of these fair rewards, would engage employees. In today's world, timely distribution of booty and benefits would create an amicable culture of recognition.

We Asians are a little different and emotional from the Western world. Here, I am emphasising to create a differentiation between performers and non-performers. In the last two decades, I have observed Asians to be not very keen to differentiate. Blame it on our culture or upbringing, or even our societal norms. On the other hand, the Western culture emphasises on methodical planning and implementation of the same.

I am sure most of you would agree with me that, we would lose high-performers, if we do not take proper care of them. Therefore, with productivity being the key for existence, one may opt for little rational and relaxed options. But there should be a definite demarcation, especially in the current economic slowdown.

Let me give you a simple example of a sales call. A lot of effort goes into collecting data, making features into advantages, and then taking it forward and making these advantages into customer's benefits. But we are too shy to ask for the cheque or closure. I have seen this across India, through my journey as a sales leader's coach. One of the key differentiators between a great salesman and good salesman is the ability to close the call on a positive note, keeping in mind our culture and our mind-set.

Similarly, it is important to reward and differentiate a performer from a non-performer.

It is good to have a value system, but it is a crime to lose a motivated, engaged, and performing resource, and thus, letting your organisation bleed. As an entrepreneurial leader, you have to be critical about what is good and required in the long run.

You would all remember the movie Spiderman. With great powers comes great responsibility. Leadership brings in responsibility to influence the thought process of followers.

The unique selling proposition of the book is that, it would deal with leadership and engagement, and therefore productivity, with different strategies for different age groups. It would also deal with the current market volatile situations.

How would it help you? It would simply help you to understand and distinguish the social characteristics of different generations, their needs, and how you would work with them. This therefore, would change the overall dynamics of how you look at different generations in your day-to-day dealings with them.

'Match the age' to 'keep them engaged' focusses on decoding the secrets of creating a happy workplace, and also beckons every people leader to focus and contribute towards their organisation by working on the following points:

- Future workplace.
- Generation difference in personality.
- Communicating with each generation effectively.
- Countering baseless myths.
- How to deal with each generation?
- Current threats and stability; their effect on engagement would be crucial.

Happy and engaged workers make happy workplaces. By employing the tips discussed in this book, we are sure to boost the morale of our workers, and keep loyalty in the company. Increased productivity and profits would follow automatically.

CHAPTER 3

Journey of 'Match the Age' to 'Keep them Engaged'

Part 1 – Change in my thoughts

The engagement data I had worked over years was at the back of my hand. I had implemented it myself at an organisational level, and hence, it was my baby. I must say, I challenged myself by choosing one of the closest topics to my heart, but also the most difficult and talked-about topic during my Doctorate Programme's research. Every leader is a born expert in people engagement. It is very difficult to further dissect this topic, as it is already widely covered. Here is when this idea struck like lightning, and the challenge became stronger.

Part 2 – Reflection of results

After collection of all the data, I started comparing, and what I saw came as a shock. I saw the engagement scores moving towards the negative side, year after year. My idea was to bring forth my professional exposure, to look at entrepreneurial leadership and engagement differently, through 'matching the age'.

Post the thesis, I further broke the scores down to age-wise matrix. I concluded that engagement requires to be looked differently for different set of age groups. I further concluded that people managers should be happy to note that engagement impacted the balance sheets.

The whopping grades I received from institutions increased my belief in the concept. The signals and the feedback of renowned leaders in business pushed me towards it, and that's how the theory was born.

Happiness is what an employee should seek from a leader. A team member always wants to be engaged and happy. This is a small desire, but we all seem to miss it.

10 Part 3 – Final results

Then came the biggest challenge to name my brain child. One evening, my wife Sayani and I, were discussing about a suitable name, and somehow, spontaneously, this came to our mind. It suited my concept aptly, and thus my child was christened.

After painful editing and re-editing, finally my book was ready to see the light. I sincerely thank Bloomsbury to be a part of my first step in the world of print media.

CHAPTER 4

'Match the Age' to 'Keep them Engaged' – Part 1

Key Objectives

- How do we 'keep them engaged'?
- Differentiate between happy and engaged employees.
- What is an engaged performance and its effect?
- People matter!
- 'Keeping them engaged': Key findings and demographic
- Importance of engaged employees.
- 'Keep them engaged': Post recruitment – a live case study.
- Role of a kind manager to 'keep them engaged'.

4.1 Basic premises of how to 'keep them engaged'?

As we began our interesting voyage, let's be open, honest, and sincere to each other. This is must for the success of the overall idea and its implementation. Let's together also commit to answer some of the not so flowery questions. I look for professionals with the right intent. It is so simple, but so uncommon in human beings.

Truth is sometimes a little bitter to digest. The faster you take steps to correct it, the better you would be, and I assure you positive results over and over again. I am committed to the truth, and that's why I have penned this down. Let's challenge the status-quo together.

Just like the role of a casting director is not over by deciding on the cast, and is required at every stage of making of the movie; similarly, a people's leader is required to be a part of every major decision, and in establishing the role of engagement interventions for his/her teams.

As we agree on it, we move on, and would firstly try and define the concept of 'keeping them engaged' (employee engagement). Let's not look at 'n' number of definitions available on Google or Wikipedia, and then jot down the available information! Let's talk straight and to the point, as I love to be different.

There is a lot of noise on what is 'keeping them engaged? There is a lot of confusion about what it exactly means. Some of the words used to define engagement in the past include, contribution, engrossment, promise, optimism, enthusiasm, or extraordinary effort.

It can be defined as a whole-hearted, passionate, and an active connection with work, which influences an employee to get across the line with excellence (because it is the work that engages the team member). Does the overall definition matches with what you have in mind?

Entrepreneurial leaders have to understand the positive signals. They should realise that it is beyond simple happiness. Engagement is more about passion and commitment, the readiness level (**Readiness level of an individual = Ability × Willingness**) to invest, and to put in an outstanding individual effort, to help the leaders succeed. They have to look for that passionate spark; fire in the right side of the anatomy. If they see one such spark in the eyes of an individual, they should ensure it is replicated, and the team member is taken care of.

Do you know, there is a huge difference between a satisfied and an engaged employee? Many entrepreneurial leaders or organisations do not understand the same. We need to clear the basic principles before we move into technical jargons; though I completely hate them, and would try and keep this approach very simple.

14

Our forefathers were happy in one job. Were they not hungry for success? Did they not think out of the box and question it? I myself do not think so. Their approach is questionable, not their intentions.

Let's look at the difference! Satisfaction denotes how a team member feels about his/her job? It may refer to remuneration and reimbursements, kitty, opportunities to progress in the organisation, overall environment, and related conditions, etc.

On the other hand, 'being engaged' denotes the state where a team member has the desire to go beyond his/her call of duty. The team members innovate, and further align with the organisation, the leader, and the individual goals. Engagement is a stage beyond job description and job specifications. It involves actions which lead to job satisfaction.

To simplify it, let's look at some examples. It can be performing extra duties without complaint, mentoring and helping subordinates, using time efficiently, sharing ideas, making suggestions for improvement, and positively representing the organisation.

If you look at modern-day organisation's behaviour studies, it is very similar to the holy book, Gita's message, which says, 'one should do his/her karmas (fundamental doctrine) without expecting any fruits or results'. It impacts in the long run by the way of increasing the organisation's effectiveness and performance. Gita rightly depicts it as 'let not the fruits of action be thy motive'.

To engage an employee first, the entrepreneurial leader needs to ensure that s/he is happy. We can definitely have a satisfied employee in our teams who is disengaged. Surprised?

There is also a dangerous state of neither being engaged nor disengaged. I call it dangerous, as it is the state where one would mostly badmouth on every opportunity, and can become disengaged in the slightest blink of an eye. These individuals are on the fence, and would jump either side, depending on the situation. Chances of negative influence is always higher in such fence sitters though.

Interestingly, leaders across the world are confused on whether they should attack these benchers, or work on disengaged people?

Should they look only at engaged workforce, and ask others to leave? There is a lot of confusion, and we would definitely try and work on it.

Do we need to use different techniques or intervention for engagement? The answer would be 'yes'! Why? Ask me…

Common sense says that, if they are different individuals, in different age groups, with different needs, then they need to be dealt differently. Isn't it? Then why not acknowledge it?

I would ask you a very simple question. Do you deal with your child, spouse, parents, friends, and not-so-good friends differently? The answer is in the question itself.

Say you are 'X' and are visiting a 'movie theatre'; and you find your best friend there. What are you going to do? Hug him/her, shake hands, smile, etc. On the contrary, if you see your boss, what would be your reaction? You would firstly ignore or avoid. If s/he has come to see a movie, you would most likely change the choice of your movie. What has happened here? The people have changed, situation is the same, but subsequently, our behaviour has also changed. Our attitude is a reflection of our behaviour with different people or situations.

Let's look at a completely different scenario. You are travelling by Rajdhani from Delhi-Mumbai. You see a shabbily dressed man standing next to you. What are you going to do? Are you going to move away? Maybe yes! As a man, you would check your wallet, your top pocket for the ticket, and also push your luggage between your feet. Won't you? Ladies would also have similar reactions. You have reacted to a stranger. Did I say he touched you? No.

Then what happens when you are snoring away to glory with 72 strangers in the compartment, without even locking the luggage? In all probability, one stranger is better than 72, just like a flight on the ground is safer than in air.

What has happened then? The situation has changed, people (strangers) are constant.

Each generation has its own core beliefs and values. It depends on political, social, and technological surroundings. We should understand their basic background, past, and principles, which reflect through their personalities. This is important for each one of the entrepreneurial leaders to communicate with the different generations in personal, as well as professional surroundings. The results? Higher employee engagement, and in-turn, better bottom line, efficiencies and effectiveness, and increased employee retention.

Entrepreneurial leaders should adopt the belief that, to put up with diverse workforces, they must understand and manage the engagement drivers and threats. The needs differ in varied age groups, thus, giving rise to different interventions.

You all would agree that 'performance management systems' and 'career prospects of team members', were viewed as the most important engagement drivers, while the reputation of the overall organisation and its Image, and the efficiency and effectiveness of its performance management systems, were viewed as the most important engagement threats.

These clearly indicate that we, as entrepreneurial leaders, need to differentiate between a performer and a non-performer. During my research, we got loads of responses on security of job and the overall organisational culture. I have kept these two parameters, keeping in mind the current economic scenario. It makes it really interesting, as youngsters are looking for organisations which contribute to the overall scheme of things (society).

4.2 Engaged performance ('keeping them engaged')

An actor gives an extraordinary performance on a day when he is fully fit, positive, and also echoes the spirits of the director and the crew. You can say so by feeling it on the screen. You can distinguish a good and a great actor from the onset of his screen presence. Getting into the skin of the character and giving an exceptional performance is something which every leader or a performer, has imbedded in his character. Consistency here is equally important as s/he has to play different roles every day. As Shakespeare says 'all the world's a stage, and all the men and women merely actors'.

There have been various powerful characters like Krishna, Draupadi, etc. They are difficult to enact, and it is difficult to get deep into the skin of these characters. It is equally difficult for the actor to come out of it. The smile of Krishna and his policies; and the power of Draupadi that you have seen on TV or in movies, is so infectious.

But do these few exceptional shots guarantee an exceptional film? These extraordinary performances should not come in fluke, or for a minute or two. They should be there, present in every minute of the movie, for it to become an exceptional piece of art.

This is the reason for the selection of a particular actor versus the role. Still, there is no guarantee that the movie is going to be a success in commercial terms.

On similar terms, constantly engaged performance can only be achieved when leaders unconditionally support their team members, and influence thought processes of followers. This would extract positive performances, aligned with the overall company's mission. Profits would follow automatically, post this alignment.

I have always put forward my thoughts that, as entrepreneurial leaders, only financially investing in the team would not help. It would be equally important to strike the right balance in which you also would be required to invest emotionally in your workforce to create the 'magic'.

I remember my visit to Disney World early this year. The engagement of the famous parade is note-worthy; the 'magic' in the air song, and everything else, is so much appreciable. How do they create the 'magic'? When employees are strategically aligned to their leaders and organisations, they contribute enthusiastically from the bottom of their hearts.

Team members also would love to be acknowledged for success. The recipe for success for an individual is straightforward.

Success = (Head + Heart) X Objectives.

As entrepreneurial leaders, we need to notice the same and work on it. Individual success would lead to the team, and indirectly, to organisational bottom line.

I recommend to each one of the leaders reading this book, importantly all decision makers, to understand and follow the Maslow's hierarchy of needs, whenever in doubt, especially in designing the interventions, or policies for the organisation. I wanted to discuss the same, and I have changed the idea off late, as I want to keep this book fresh in thoughts. Please refer to the same. It takes a minute. Let's carry on…

I firmly believe that as a people's leader, your objectives, commitments, and intentions, should always be right, to achieve success.

I sometimes feel that leaders miss out on basic essentials of entrepreneurial leadership and engagement, and normally work on high-end interventions. I have seen entrepreneurial leaders do well overall, when it comes to providing solutions for higher level of needs, maybe because their needs are different from their subordinates'. Empathise with them by putting yourself in their situation, which must have been similar to yours in the past. Instrumentally, they are very happy with great scores of frill or high-end questions. They feel very uncomfortable to agree and provide support to the action plan for basic needs.

It is a famous story. Once everyone was looking at a big rock and there was the great Michelangelo also present. People were asked what they saw. They said a rock. Michelangelo, when asked, said that he could see a very powerful horse. He picked up his chisel and started working on it. The rest is history.

Different perspectives in life are similar to different needs. Entrepreneurial leaders need to be like Michelangelo, and should try and make a horse out of a rock. You should be able to chisel out the dirt from the sides of the rock, and trim it to make every employee your powerful horse.

We all have seen a very famous movie Paa. I must accolade here the thought process and the vision of the director. The casting director took the real-life father to play the son's role, and the real-life son to play the father's role. I call it an extraordinary vision.

It is in no-way an offence to anyone, but challenging the status-quo, based on the potential of the respective actors, he made a piece of art. It will remain with us till we exist.

Let's look at one of the real-time examples from my professional world to make it simple. One of my CEO's in a steel manufacturing plant, distributed to his supervisors, books on safety and other related stuff, for the star performance of the month. Can you guess where the books landed up the next morning? Yes, on my table. As a corporate human resource head, they requested me for vouchers worth the price of the books, or of some retail store? It would be more useful to us, they emphasised. It was not the intent which is doubtful here. It is the need of the employee which was different. He, as a leader, just needs to empathise with the employees, and then provide solutions.

So, taking a clue from the examples and our discussions, we need to first work on the basic questions like, 'Is the employee aware of the management's expectations from him/her?' and 'Does s/he, has the right tools, to complete his/her job in the best possible manner (quality and quantity wise)?'

One very interesting incident happened when I was getting trained by *Gallup on Q 12* and employee engagement. One of the participants, who was a human resource leader, shared with us his strategy to engage with a new joinee.

He said, he called all new joinees after they had accepted the offer letter. He would explain to them how their day would look like. What sort of pressures they needed to deal with, and most importantly, the new joinees were explained the expectations from the job, leaders, and the organisation.

He continued saying that, it was a big shock to his leaders, as the join-to-hire ratio decreased. It hit an all-time low of 40 per cent. On the other hand, his attrition in the team was close to zero per cent. Once a team member joins the leader, knowing what is expected out of him, what pressures he needs to deal with, he is mentally prepared to work with this leader.

It is an interesting and different perspective from an entrepreneurial leader. A cup of coffee with the new employee, made a lot of difference.

It is always nice to have good figures for top-end, but it would be disastrous in the heat of the moment to ignore bad scores at the bottom of the pyramid. Always, pyramids are built from the bottoms up, with a strong foundation. Same is the case with any other hierarchy of need or engagement module.

My overall outlook is to first stick to the basics, and then move ahead. People leaders, please do not make a mistake here. I have pointed it out quite a number of times, and therefore, I hope each one of you would understand the importance of it. I have also tried and explained to you the above with loads of examples, so that we are on the same page. Penning down these thoughts is just to ensure that, as individuals, your learning opportunities increase.

Similarly, in a movie, you need to extraordinarily work throughout the three hours. For that, you need months and years of hard work, day-in and out.

To 'keep them engaged', you need to ask yourself as an entrepreneurial leader, the simple questions at the organisational and individual level:-

Engage #1   If the employees are not given a clear key result area or key performance indicators, or not given proper tools, to complete his/her job in a best possible manner, how would they perform? Is the employee aware of the management's expectations from him/her (quality and quantity wise)? Would they then be benefited from a top of the end intervention, like a career path?

(KRA: Key Result Area and KPI: Key Performance Indicator. What do I need to do, and what will I be measured on, respectively)

Engage #2   What motivates which category of employees?

Engage #3   Is there a gap in your organisation plan v/s individual needs?

Engage #4   What sort of a rewards and recognitions would be more effective?

The questions are very similar to those of a casting director. The role, plot, story, capabilities of actors, their chemistry, director's strength, music, etc., are all vital to make a block buster, and thus, it is to be ensured that all the wheels are well-oiled.

4.3 People matter

I remember the great man, Mr P R S Oberoi always saying, 'people are the key differentiators. You may replicate our hotels and products, but you wouldn't be able to replicate the people whom we train'. How many things did the Oberoi's pioneer? The Oberoi centre of learning and development, in-room dinning service, women house keepers, wake-up calls, etc.

These were the amenities which they gave to their guests, but now have become in-built features in all hotels. Maybe his people are the only reason that their 4–6 hotels feature in any top 10 lists of hotels across the globe, let alone India. Fortunately, I have seen it very closely in my career.

I have the highest regards for Mr Oberoi, and I stand to be a firm believer of what he has said. No doubt about it. Please forgive me sir, when I say that in today's concept, it is not only people, but good and engaged people, who are our key assets. With such poor scores of fully engaged team members, it is a must to have good and engaged workers, and not just mere workers.

Have a look around? The difference is noticeable even if there are two or more organisations delivering similar services, or manufacturing the same product. What makes one company more successful than the other? Have you asked yourself? What is so different? Packaging? Better quality of merchandise or produce, better services, more specific and streamlined strategies, state-of-the-art technologies, or better pricing?

All the above are continuously contributing to superior performance, but all of them can be copied over time. One thing that differentiates a market leader from a market challenger or a market follower is its good people. Do you agree as an entrepreneurial leader? It is proven over time that engaged employees are more productive and efficient.

In these testing times, every leadership team should have one goal that is productivity, which can improve through engagement. The fight for trained manpower and also trainable manpower is equal in the service or the manufacturing sectors, and the trained manpower is very scarce. 90 per cent of the current pass outs are unemployable as per MASCOM. Also, every batch is superior to the previous, ensuring the skills are redundant every three years. What is then a constant? It is the people management and behavioural skills which are constant over the last thousand years, and would always be constant. This is what you are fired for 90 per cent of the times, though in the beginning you were hired for your ability (knowledge and skill) and not your attitude (willingness or behaviour).

Entrepreneurial mind-set in leaders should not allow the competition an opportunity at all. All of you, I am sure, would hate it, if you lose your high performing team member to a competitor. If so, then you need to sweat it out for them.

Good leaders always produce good leaders, but not-so-good and scared leaders, only produce followers.

> We need to realise what good salesmen do across the world. They differentiate between features, ascertain the advantages, and then convert them into the benefits for customers. It may differ from customer to customer, even for the same product. Eventually, a feature may not sell, but benefits do. For example, we use mobile phones with hundreds of features, but the benefit of the mobile phone can be calls, emails, social networking, or anything else, depending on our needs. It is different for you and me, even if we use the same handset.
>
> A good salesman also ensures the closure of deals, by asking for money or signing for commitments.

Likewise, all our organisational-level interventions should be beneficial for our people. You, as an entrepreneurial leader, need to answer a simple question: If you were an employee and I would sell an engagement calendar, or say any other intervention like a training plan, or a reward and recognition scheme, new PMS, productivity charts, etc., would you buy it for ₹ 1000/- off the shelf like you do with a credit card? Why not? Are you habitual of taking free benefits?

Anyone would like to have an engagement/training/OD calendar (or any other intervention, or reward) free of cost. Would they purchase it? If I would have to add a price tag to it, what's the answer likely to be? No. Then change the plan, but if your answer is yes, kindly go

24

ahead. You are on the right path my friend. It has to be attractive. 'Jo dikhta hai who bikhta hai', which can be loosely translated to visibility sells, or eye level is the buy level.

Have you looked at what really drives employee engagement? The few key drivers of engagement (to 'keep them engaged'), not in any particular order are:

Engage #1   Association with the organisation.

Engage #2   Tuning with the direct superior.

Engage #3   Contentment towards leaders.

Engage #4   Safety at work.

Engage #5   Overall contribution to the society, surprisingly in most youngsters.

The last two drivers have increased the number of responses in the last five years or so.

4.4 Key findings: 'keeping them engaged'

Let's look at the clue from some of the key data derived out of global surveys, and my analysis of Indian organisations of repute:

Engage #1   It is alarming that less than 15 per cent of the employees are fully engaged across the globe, so there is a need to 'keep them always engaged'. In India, the numbers are close to 9–10 per cent only, which is a bigger challenge.

Engage #2   Approximately 25 per cent of the employees are disengaged across the globe, and in India, the same has increased to approximately 30 per cent.

Engage #3   Approximately 60 per cent of the employees across the globe are on the bench. They are partially engaged with the need to 'keep themselves towards the status of being engaged' and move it towards the right path or direction.

Like the director keeps re-taking the shot till it's perfect to his/her satisfaction, and the potential of the actor, we need to keep emphasising on this as entrepreneurial leaders.

My figures and global survey/s were +/- 1 per cent variant. So I have kept them constant here.

Engage #4   Gender, type of job, roles and responsibilities, and industries or trade, do not emerge as a critical variable of engagement

Engage #5   Engagement was found more in senior management of large corporations. They distinctly have a college education, and they earn more than ₹10 lakh per annum in the Indian scenario. They are mostly older employees.

Engage #6   Youngsters, most highly educated, and lower income level employees, were found with the least level of engagement. Newer employees, who had spent less than 1 year, client facing or clerical staffers, telephone handlers, those working in manufacturing and waste management (based on the nature of the job), etc., have the lowest identified levels of engagement. Thus, it is important for the overall organisational success to 'keep them engaged', especially for front-end employees.

These front-end employees are the source of connect between you, the organisation, and the customers. If they are so important for the overall success, it won't be wrong if we take special care of them.

Think about it! Have you ever called a call centre simply to appreciate their efforts? Have we ever stopped and thanked the waiter who served us on December 31 (New Year eve)?

4.5 Key indicators

I will keep on reminding you of these figures, so that you know the seriousness of what I say next. I recommend people leaders reading the next few facts, to please read it at least a couple of times, before moving ahead.

Indicator #1 One of the top five needs of the hour stated by leaders in India, is employee and talent engagement, and through it, retention of key talent. Do you all agree? I second the thoughts of the leaders who have given me this input. Even research across the world throws up these in the top five needs. Though I do not agree with some of the leaders who think that engagement is a tool to reduce attrition, it is more than that.

Indicator #2 Next is a bomb shell. Open your eyes friends. Surprisingly, 50 per cent of the organisations do not have a talent retention and engagement plan. Isn't this surprising? It is not only in Indian companies, but MNC's as well.

Indicator #3 More than 60 per cent of global organisations do not have a human resource plan.

Indicator #4 The bomb itself; one out of every three engaged employees is looking for a job in India. So, it becomes 33 out of 100 employees. In disengaged employees, this should be close to 100 per cent. It means that, 33 per cent of high performers and highly engaged talent are looking for a new job in India. Wow! I am really amazed. What are we people leaders doing?

Indicator #5   The more shocking fact is that, it is up by three times in the last five years. We are looking at one of the youngest workforces across the globe in a few years from now. Do you think, as a people's leader, it's time to act? Can we think pro-actively? Otherwise, where are we heading to?

Indicator #6   64 per cent of the high performers are disengaged across the globe. Come on now! You all must be wondering that this is plain exaggeration. However, this is a fact, reiterated by Discovery, a famous institute based out of Scotland. The studies I conducted threw a similar figure, with 3 per cent variance from the above.

4.6 Demographics: 'keeping them engaged'

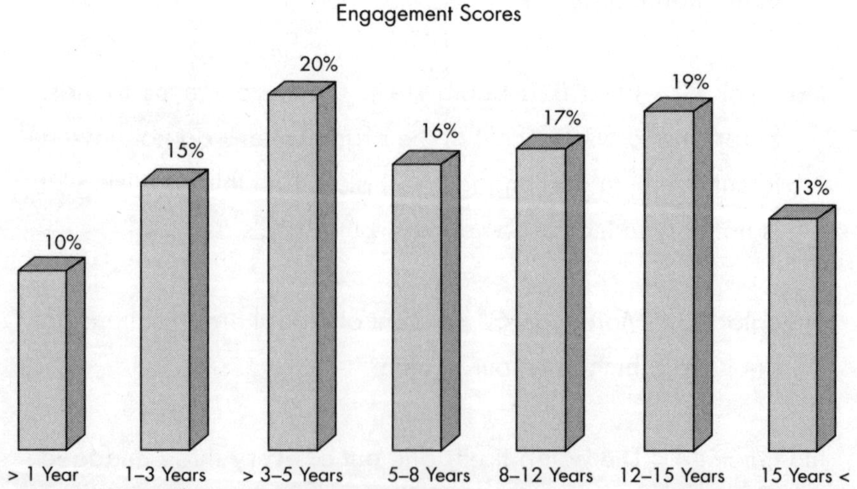

Engagement Scores

FIGURE 4.1   Percentage of engaged employees based on the number of years of service

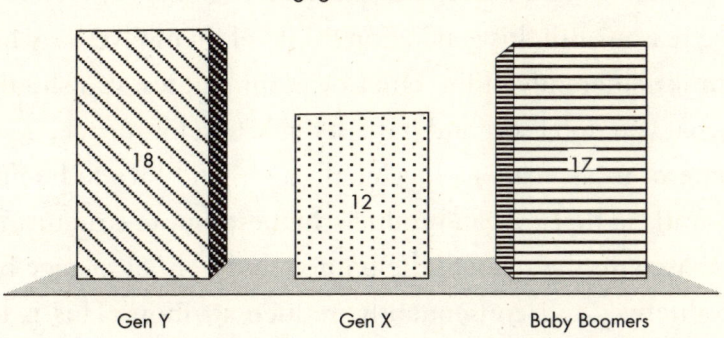

Engagement Scores

Gen Y   Gen X   Baby Boomers

FIGURE 4.2   Percentage of engaged employees based on generations

Taking a clue from the facts, we can visualise from Figures 4.1 and 4.2 above that, engaging employees for entrepreneurial leaders would become more and more challenging. The scores have drastically come down from the range of 25s to 15s in the last few years. Similarly, expectations have gone up. It is not merely a few games, a birthday celebration, etc., which are going to help you. It is an honest intent, followed by a concrete action plan, which may support you.

In Figure 4.1, you see the rise of score in the middle ages, and then again, a sudden dip in the engagement level. In the Indian scenario, whether you call it the current generation's outlook or the modernisation effect, it can be visibly seen that employees start disengaging, or the graph dips twice, once approximately post five years, and the next, post 10–12 years of continuous service. You would have agreed with me when I said 33 out 100 employees are looking for 'a' job. A job here means even a different job in the same organisation or a different organisation as a whole.

It is very important for a people leaders to study these trends. If you compare it with Figure 4.2, it is quite obvious that the generation mostly reading this book, falling in the middle management, is the biggest contributor to this downfall.

It is quite interesting, and I wish to pen it down. From my studies, it was evident that team members, down the line, were not so critical of each other or their bosses, but the team members of Gen X were. Is it the reason? But this generation thinks of themselves very highly, and thinks differently of the other two. Sometimes, you should not trust what you don't see, and it was a big lesson for me too.

Some of us, as leaders, love challenges, and love to be pushed to the wall, so that we can produce the best; but re-structuring our needs based on the need of the hour would help us engage better, be productive, and consequently, reduce attrition. This is how I expect the leaders with an entrepreneurial instinct to react to the above figures.

4.7 The importance of 'keeping them engaged'

In the case of making of a movie, the whole cast is engaged/aligned to the project till the very end. They behave, dress, and act their parts, even when they come to promote their movie on a TV show. Give it a thought. What could be the exact reason for the same?

Keeping in mind the current scenario, many leaders say, change is permanent, or we should learn to live in our lives with uncertainty, etc. Some of you reading the book would be more active followers of these leaders on social media. In the current market, it would not be wrong if I say, employee engagement and loyalty are more vital than ever before to an organisation's success and competitive advantage. Still, do we have a concrete plan for the same? The answer would be no in most cases. Why is this so? As entrepreneurial leaders, have we thought about the same? It's time to put on our thinking caps.

Gone are the days when a young person joined a company and stayed there until retirement. In today's business environment, there are no guarantees. It is predicted that current employees below 30 years of age, will have 10–15 employments in their lifecycle of employment. We have come a long way when our fathers joined as apprentices, and retired from the same organisations. It is now acceptable to have a few changes in your resume, and it is not considered as a one life, one employment theory. But to cut it short, I think, if an employee is engaged to the job and the organisation for a long period, and remains positively contributing, I would not mind it as a leader. It is healthier than having a disengaged employee.

In today's scenario, we want contribution from day 1, and we want 24X7 service. When you are a customer, you demand it. The same is the demand of your customer too. It can be internal or external, and can be paid or be a free service.

I have been to various seminars, spoken at various forums, and I see many leaders in today's world talk about the need for employable (skills) employees. The need for the skills and on-the-job training is normally mentioned by seven out of 10 leaders. No offense intended to these leaders, but if you are not an MBA or highly educated, the same seven out of 10 companies in India would outrightly reject you. These are the companies where the leaders need to 'walk the talk' and clearly state what they need. Also, it would be important when we are thinking about engagement, that we think of what our employees feel and need over and above every other issue. This is the priority.

With due respect to each one of those learned friends, leaders, and human resource colleagues, isn't it time to look at somewhere inside us? Once, I was speaking to a senior bureaucrat. We both agreed that 20 years of experience in the professional world is equivalent to a doctorate degree. Have you ever thought of inducting the top executives into education? Some of these top executives are brilliant, and kids would love them. They would learn more and practically from them. It is high time we include them and let them contribute in the tune of 30–40 per cent, through their practical knowledge. Let the other half remain with the academicians. This would also dish out more employable or skilled workforce. I feel this is the major difference between progressions of some countries, including Asia Pacific, though our first biggest challenge is population.

Experts predict the turnover rates to rise over 65 per cent in hospitality, customer care, ITES, and other allied industries. I second the same. But what are we doing about it? Only talent management and engagement plan, and its implementation, can help us. We have already stated that half of the companies don't believe in it.

I also second leaders when they say that the training cost and the cost of wrong recruitment, etc., totals up to 20 per cent extra costs. A concrete plan would help us to recruit and train the right person for the right job.

Therefore, the ability to engage and retain valuable employees has a very deep impact on an organisation's bottom line, apart from telling the world that they care for their employees.

We also know that, in the current scenario, one wrong thing we do as leaders would be on Facebook or Twitter in the next 24 hours, with 1000 comments and likes. One good thing we do would also be on social media, and we will have 10 odd positive references. The ideal ratio, is 9:81 in terms of positive v/s negative reach across the planet.

The question for entrepreneurial leaders is, how to ensure that the people supervisors interact with individuals to generate an engaged workforce? Why I have mentioned supervisors is because, they are your thread, and are the real champions, and your eyes and ears, especially in large organisations or manufacturing set-ups.

> Mark Zuckerberg once said that, 'Do not hire people post 30, because they lose the zest'. Welcome to the gang sir, as you are now 30 plus. It is now time for you to be called Gen X, and your employability is also at stake, as per your own words.

In my overall exposure, I have seen people leaving mostly in the first three months of their new employment, which hurts me the most. You spend a lot of time, money, and energy, only to find in first three months that s/he is not performing.

You know the brilliant alumni of IIT's or IIM's whom we hire, have a life span of 8–9 months, before they decide to quit. Do we need to stop going to these institutes? Or do we need to look at something else?

In a majority of instances, the employee, while in the recruitment stage, was made to feel great, but when on-board was neglected. The leaders had no time even to induct him, meet with him, and have a cup of coffee. He mostly felt disengaged, and not welcomed into the new family.

Have you even been to a wedding of a relative, where you were not welcomed? Remember that day, and equate it to the new joiners experience, and you will know the answer.

As people's leaders, we should not do this to the talent we have hired with so much difficultly. In this world, it is difficult to get a right fit, and if we have hired someone, we should ensure due diligence. S/he then should be a treasure for you as a leader.

It is not only the cost of recruitment I am bothered about, but it is the vision of leaders, the culture of the organisation, and the overall core value of the leadership, which worries me the most.

When I see a star student from a premier college, or a top performer, used as an EA to the chairman or the MD, it reflects to me the top management's or the leader's overall thinking and attitude in the organisation. I have seen many times a high-potential or a fast-track trainee made to struggle, because s/he is an exceptional talent. It's time to admire it and use their talent to improve productivity. It is your organisation, and if they can impact it better, then they should be treated more fairly.

I have always believed that engaging people through innovative induction, and first three months of hand holding, helps the overall organisation in a big way.

As discussed earlier, engagement and talent retention was considered as one of the top five key challenges by leaders, where 50 per cent of these organisations, did not even have a concrete plant for the same. Isn't this alarming? I have pointed it twice in quick succession, so that we realise where we are heading to!

4.8 Importance of 'keeping them engaged': learning from a live example

In one of my very interesting assignments and responsibilities, I was assigned the task to take care of operational trainees in a hotel company. I was told by the general manager to work on the offer v/s join ratios. We had to hire 300 team members to get to a final figure of 100 new joinees. This was a shear waste of our time, energy, and resources.

After taking over the role and checking all facts and figures, I realised we were selecting the best of the lot, hitting the campus first, and we had the best brand too. Then what was missing?

After a lot of brainstorming, we couldn't find a solution. The answer was finally discovered by me in the middle of the night, while studying the data repeatedly. It was common sense that we were not engaging with them after rolling out offers for the next 5–6 months. So anyone, who had no more offers or had no good brand, joined us; the rest of them took better offers, or chose engaging companies or leaders.

Post taking over and putting everything in order, I made a 5-point-connect – let's name it the 'Keep them Engaged' programme, which to be honest, was considered non-sensual by a few of my team members, and the leadership of the hotel. Thankfully, the person who mattered the most supported and encouraged the plans; my then general manager. Thank you Mr Rai. We both sat down and put up the pointers as mentioned below. Thus, I changed my overall career in people leadership through engagement.

Since then, I stuck to it, as I always do, when I believe in someone or something:

Engage #1:   Wish every offered candidate on their birthdays by sending a personalised card signed by leaders with a bouquet of flowers.

Engage #2:   Created a brand by making inaugural presentations (first year) and final presentations in various colleges. Started making connects with all A-grade colleges.

Engage #3:   Wished each one of the selected team members for their exams. Asked them and helped them if they needed any help at the time of their exams. Opportunities to practice and train at the hotel in the evening before exams were opened up. Faculty of the institutes were encouraged to come and understand the out of box innovations.

Engage #4:   Invited them to all activities like parties, picnics, annual day, etc. They were already connected with the organisation at this stage.

Engage #5:   Invited their parents to visit the hotel, show around, and meet me and their direct managers. Created a parental set-up.

Result: Offer – joining ratio jumped to 72 per cent.

4.8.1 Learnings derived from 'keeping them engaged'

Common sense is so uncommon in human beings, and if you believe in something, just follow with your heart and head. It is not only important that we recruit or induct the right people in a right way, and for the right job, but it is equally important that we look at other activities or mid-term connects, which may change the overall thought process and results.

You may use this as learning for all your management trainees, graduate engineer trainees, or any other programmes too, as I have seen most of the large companies being disconnected here. They are sometimes overconfident of the brand, which they should be, but entrepreneurial leaders always look for bettering the ratios.

Students in the top bracket in good colleges are looking for an opportunity with an organisation where they are contributing, and it is reflected by the presentations recruiters make in their campuses. My overall view in this regard is very simple. Send your best man for the job; a person who can convert the company's vision into what these young kids dream. But, whatever you promise on the platform, deliver it. Pre-plan, discuss, and then hit the campus before committing. I had once handled such a mess, by whomever, burning my hands completely. I learnt a lot from the incident. It was difficult to clear the mess created by my predecessor and the management. My advice to leaders is to under promise when you sit with these young kids and over deliver your promise.

4.9 The Role of a 'manager' to 'keep them engaged'

An overall 'kind' attitude and the positive intent of entrepreneurial leaders is one of the key elements that drives engagement (keeps them engaged). Team members always love their leaders, if they care about their personal lives. Everyone wants to be treated as a person, and not as an asset; we in our lives treasure friendship the most. A people manager's ability to support them, enquire about their well-beings, involve their families, and with this, build strong unbreakable bonds, would count more and more in the decades to come.

Gone are the days of team approach. Nowadays, leaders are expected to build team interaction, but move away from a 'team focussed' approach, to more of an 'individual focussed' (from 1 to many towards 1 to 1) approach, which creates a healthy environment for team members to perform at the highest levels. You would agree that when there is an emotional connect, trust levels are also high, and this is of utmost importance.

Whenever I have conducted an engagement survey, whether it was *Gallup survey* or a self-designed survey, one of the most debatable questions was on a leader's feeling, when they asked, 'why do we need to have a question on the best pal at work?' The subsequent questions which arose in various forums were, 'why do I need to care? S/he is not my best mate, so how do I share my secrets or other issues which are personal?'

I am a firm preacher of emotional connect. When in any relationship, be it husband and wife, student and teacher, boss and subordinate, there is a definite emotional connect and trust. If any one of the two breaks, it becomes completely unrepairable. I hope I can take you all 10–15 years back into history. Were you aware of how you wanted to be treated when you were 20–22 years old? Were you needing all the handholding and guiding, or were you all born geniuses? Did you get such favourable climate? If you didn't, it doesn't mean that they will not create a healthy climate for their current subordinates. We should together ensure that these kids don't face

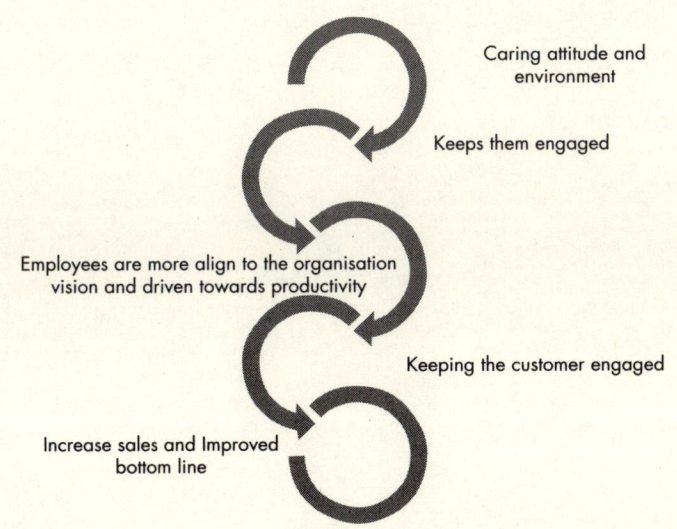

Caring attitude and environment

Keeps them engaged

Employees are more align to the organisation vision and driven towards productivity

Keeping the customer engaged

Increase sales and Improved bottom line

FIGURE 4.3   Role of the manager in 'keeping them engaged'

what we faced in the beginning of our careers. We all are educated and should behave like an educated mass, and a considerate class of people.

In the next chapter, we would try setting up the tone, and look for reasons why everyone is not engaged; what we need to ensure is to keep them engaged.

Key Learnings

Satisfaction denotes how a team member feels about his job. It may be due to remuneration, opportunities to progress, overall environment or any related condition. Engagement is a state where a team member desires to go beyond the call of duty. Performance management systems and career prospects of the team members were viewed as the most important engagement drivers.

Good and engaged people are our key assets. Fully engaged scores globally are less than 15 per cent and comparative scores in Indian context are close to 9 per cent. This is quite alarming. In India, team members earning more than 10 lakh per annum are more engaged. Leaders in the long run should build team interaction and move from 'team focussed' approach while designing interventions, to a more 'individual focussed' approach.

CHAPTER 5

'Match the Age' to 'Keep them Engaged' – Part 2

Key Objectives

- Organisational Judgements.
- Will 'keeping them engaged' deliver results?
- Why everyone isn't fully engaged?
- Measuring how to 'keep them engaged'?
- Existing measures available.
- Variations in how to 'keep them engaged'?
- Brief steps of 'keeping them engaged'.
- Moving employees to a higher level of engagement.
- Outcomes of 'keeping them engaged': organisational and employee level.

5.1 Organisational judgements

Every entrepreneurial leader reading this book would agree with me, that performance level of teams either makes or breaks any organisation's strategy. If good people are a key source of competitive advantage, their engagement, apart from performance, should also be equally important to you. It would hit directly at the numbers on the balance sheet. Ultimately, delivering strategy is about hiring the right people for the right job (right-fit) and motivating them to deliver results.

I met an interesting CEO, can't name him, sometime back. I was, at that time, eagerly looking for a role back in my home town. He spoke about productivity, and I spoke about productivity through engagement. He told me nothing is important in an organisation but numbers. I totally agree. I have no doubt it does. But at what expense? Eventually, I realised his concepts were not something which matched mine. I couldn't join him, though the offer was very lucrative. I have never worked for only hiring and firing.

Good people are your key assets, but can't be treated over matrices or like other assets. I say, throw out those matrices and concentrate on people. Results would follow suit. They will give you more than what you can think of. Even in the most difficult times, 41 per cent of the engaged employees feel that they will stick with the companies even in bad times, for it has stood by them, when they needed it. Think over it! I leave you with these thoughts…

A casting director and similarly entrepreneurial leaders need to answer the following important questions:

Match #1   Who would fit in? Which actor would help the movie to succeed? Who can fit into the role aptly? What types of people will help the organisation to succeed?

Match #2   What do I want from these set of actors? Why would the best people I need for my business want to work here?

Match #3   How should we treat our people so they deliver peak performance time and time again? How should the director manage and treat their actors?

Match #4   And finally, what would be best for the movie or the organisation?

It is important to plan and answer all what's, who's, and why's of life?

These questions cut to the heart of engaged performance, which I firmly believe are the factors that would be the key differentiators, enabling organisational judgements, and would be part of your future plans on engaging teams.

A recent survey of investors showed that 35 per cent of their decisions are now hinged on non-financial factors. It is an indication? It shows us the path in terms of enormousness. Investors feel towards organisation's leaders and their capability to encourage team members and ensure a 'magical' experience for the customer.

Entrepreneurial leaders are therefore, encouraged not to ignore the fundamentals of engagement, particularly in these difficult times. It is important that a proper due perfectionism is attributed to the same.

If you look at bright young talents around, you will see they are more or less equal to these investors, investing in their talents. When they walk out of their comfort zones, to a completely different world of methods, they are often found confused and clueless. It is, therefore, suggested that we handle them with utmost care from day 1.

5.2 Will 'keeping them engaged' deliver improved business results?

There are many studies which are available across the globe, which prove that 'keeping them engaged' delivers improved business results. One of them is the analysis of *America's most admired companies*. The direct result of pro-employee measures was in the form of stock movement by 50 per cent over the challengers.

It is proved through various studies that engaged teams produce better results. Even upshot of companies with similar products or services can vary based on engagement levels of their employees. Let us look at a very simple example of a restaurant. There are many restaurants selling the same cuisine, and catering to different clientele. They may deliver similar products but their service or standards differ. Here, people contribute to the differentiator, thus, helping the organisation and teams to win continually.

There are many such examples with a measurable return on investment, and we are going to discuss a few of them.

In many forums or conferences, where I have spoken on employee engagement, entrepreneur or entrepreneurial leaders always ask me, will 'keeping them engaged' drive productivity? The answer is yes! Of course it does. Is it measurable? I am a strong preacher of the same!

Any intervention can be measured, and the results also tells us its return on investment. It will definitely impact, tangibly or intangibly, think about it. Something or the other will always move in a positive direction. It can be quality scores, sales, production index, customer satisfaction, or attrition. It has to, or else you should stop the exercise. It is a waste of time as we all need to think like an entrepreneurial leaders and improve numbers.

It is sometimes easier to measure these movements in scores, in production or manufacturing-driven industries. Directly, the number and the bottom line moves. But definitely, some matrix or number moves directly, or indirectly in service industries as well. It is these challenges which make you a better leader.

> The gross profit earned in the market by the movie is the return of investment for the producer. The producer has, from day 1, a budget, and follows the same, penny by penny. I would also recommend entrepreneurial leaders to measure the return of investment for every intervention, and sell it to business/customers. Don't just be a follower, but be an initiator who can make an impact. We sometimes need to sell ourselves in this world of competition through facts and figures. That's the key to move ahead.

It would be surprising for me if any of my readers would walk into the boss's chamber and directly inform him/her about what s/he can expect from the subordinate in the next three months. It is very important to plan your short-term and long-term goals. A good leader always keeps his/her goals dynamic and flexible with the situation. Adaptability is the key to success.

Organisational effectiveness research scientists have proved that among the manufacturing set-ups, the organisations which have good manufacturing practices (GMP), would account for about 18 per cent improvement in productivity. This may lead to more than 20 per cent positive upshot. It was clearly evident in the studies that people management practices are a better indicator of company's presentation than approach, expertise, or progressions.

People work towards various certifications like ISO, OSHAS, SA8000, HACCP, IQA, Green Belt, and CMMI levels, just to build that culture and drill. Overall, these processes make you more robust and competitive.

We can identify many motivational drivers that help create an engaged workplace, and influence results as an entrepreneurial leader.

They are majorly value system of an organisation, superiority in relation to competition, opportunities to learn and grow through career progression, aiding environment which continually supports performance, work and life balance, and measurable, timely and attainable booty month on month.

Entrepreneurial leaders should note that all of these drivers will matter equally to everyone. We need to identify the most significant needs within the diverse segments of our workforce, post identification of an 'ideal employee'.

These 'ideal employees' need definite plans, as the workforces are diverse in nature. People leaders can only then help design efficient interventions to meet individual needs of team members, and effectively engage them. One-size-fits-all no longer works as an organisational strategy. We need to have different plans, as our workforces are diverse in nature, and so are their needs.

5.2.1 Engaged performance model

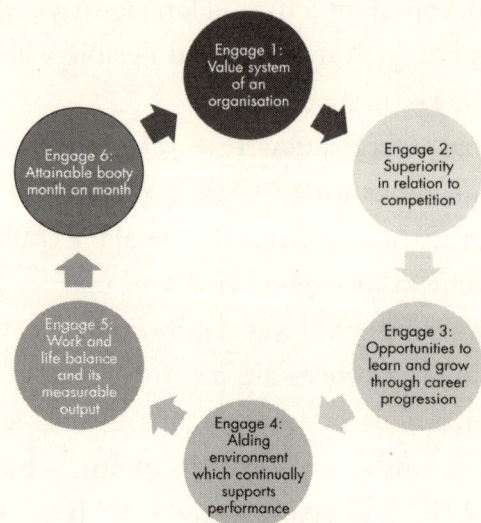

FIGURE 5.1   Engaged performance model ('keep them engaged ')

5.2.2 Six elements of engaged performance model

Please note these six elements can be clubbed together with the following sub-traits:

Engage #1   Value system of the organization.

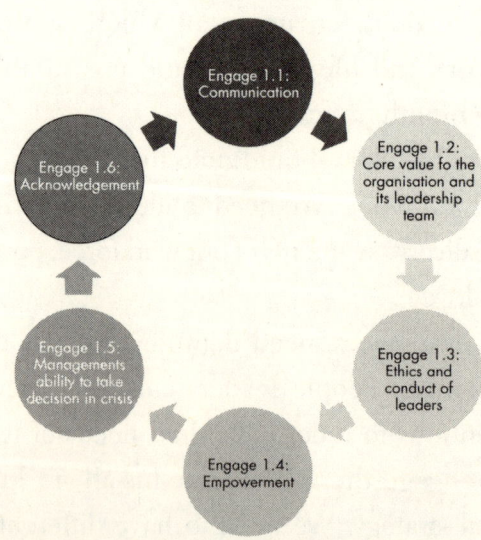

FIGURE 5.2   Value system of the organization

46

Engage #2   Superiority in relation to competition.

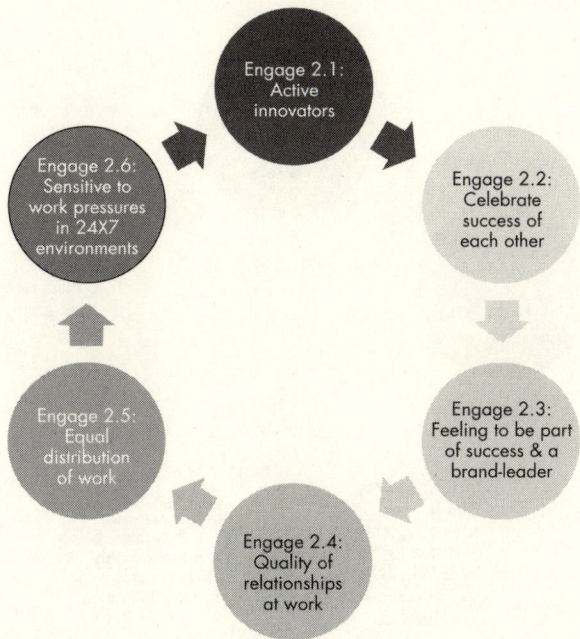

FIGURE 5.3   Superiority in relation to competition

Engage #3   Opportunities to learn and grow through career progression.

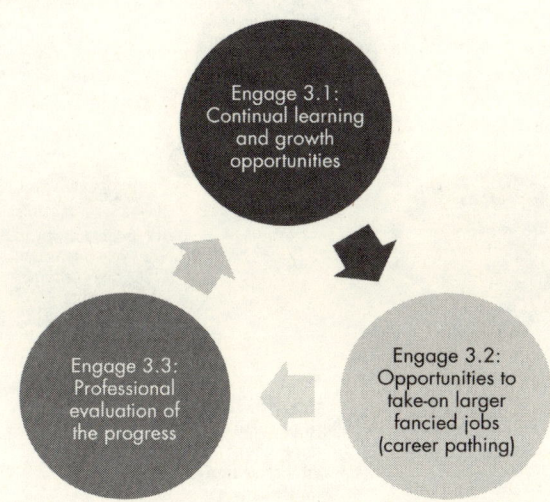

FIGURE 5.4   Opportunities to learn and grow through career progression

Engage #4 Aiding environment which continually supports performance.

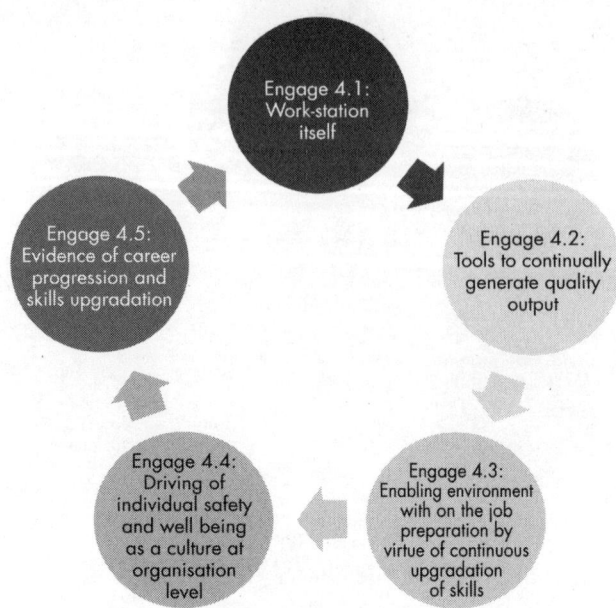

FIGURE 5.5   Aiding environment which continually supports performance

Engage #5   Work and life balance.

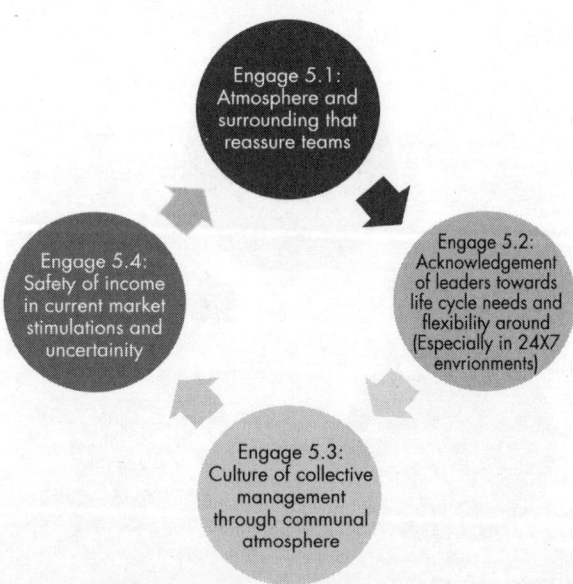

FIGURE 5.6   Work and life balance

Engage #6   Measurable and attainable booty month on month.

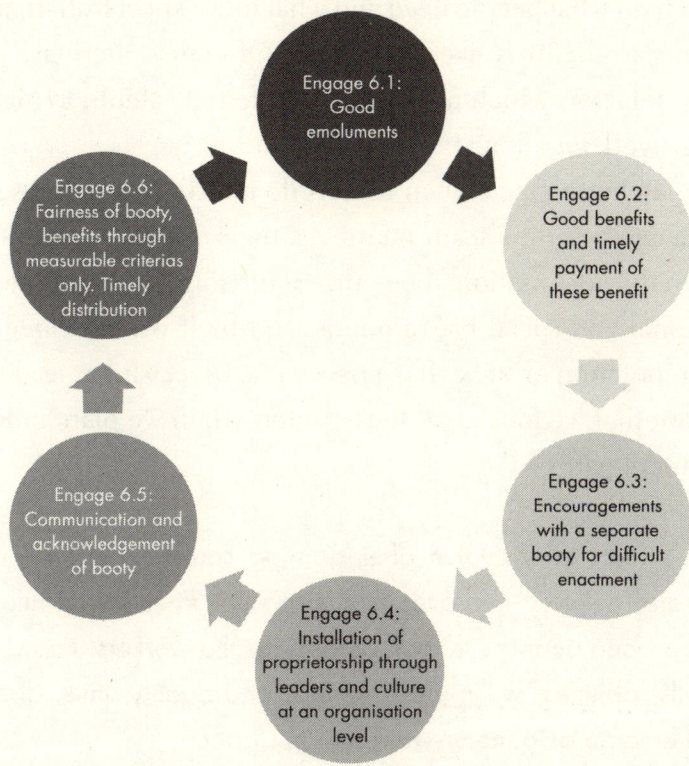

FIGURE 5.7   Measurable and attainable booty month on month

5.3 Why isn't then everyone 'fully engaged'?

Why are all movies not super hits? Why do sometimes the best actors fail? Why all movies with big stars don't make it to the 100 crore league? Do you think they don't put their best into it? Then why are some successful, while others fail?

It can be anything; a not so strong story line, non-commercial music or unappealing location, average performance of good actors, or bad directorial ventures can sometimes be a cause. The success on the other hand can be due to a hit song, great locations, and outstanding performance of the actor or the director. You never know, there is no set formula of success.

Similarly, when we speak about organisations, there can be a mismatch on what people need and what they expect from their jobs. According to me, it is like a marriage. Of course there are a large number of factors which may affect in different extents, to make this marriage work for a long period of time.

Mismatches happen when leaders do not study trends associated with the ageing of the team members, their overall experience and tenure in the organisation, their current life stage and priorities, their educational and social backgrounds, and their overall career stage and its reputation or stake. If we have to be successful as leaders, it is important that we look at all these factors when we plan 'individual engagement paths'.

> Actors mature and evolve after gaining some experience. Their talent and delivery improves with exposure to realty. Similarly, a well-seasoned people's leader, recognises the workers' knowledge; his skills, abilities, willingness, speed, and quality, thus, directing him to emerge as a mature and fine performer.

'Match the age' reflects on the realty how a job once preferred becomes a mismatch over a period of time, to the same individual. Reverse is also equally applicable. It is therefore important for an entrepreneurial leader to assess the age bracket of the team members, and then come up with a solution. It is always better to do it in a customised manner, rather than doing the damage control later.

Job mismatch can have significant short and long-term consequences. Entrepreneurial leaders should know with experience that when expectations are not fulfilled, employees may disengage from work. This would evidently show in their productivity, and they would be in office only for their pay package. They would not only leave the organisation when an employment situation arises, but would also leave no stone unturned to move engaged resources into a disengaged one.

Sometimes, the cost of bad recruitment and its repelling effect are very high, especially if the employee is a youngster. They are well-connected and the news can spread like wild fire, whether good or bad. Therefore, entrepreneurial leaders should always look at 'matching the age' and 'keeping them engaged'.

5.4 If employers offer quality employment experiences to their employees, will all employees remain engaged?

If we simply look at what drives engagement at the workplace, we will note that emoluments and designation, or the overall role might affect the verdict to join an organisation. But factors such as opportunities for learning and development are related towards engagement, wherein, an employee goes the extra mile to create that 'magic'.

If we look at factors that attract, retain, and engage teams, we can list down easily a few important pointers:

Engage #1   Factors that attract the right talent or people.

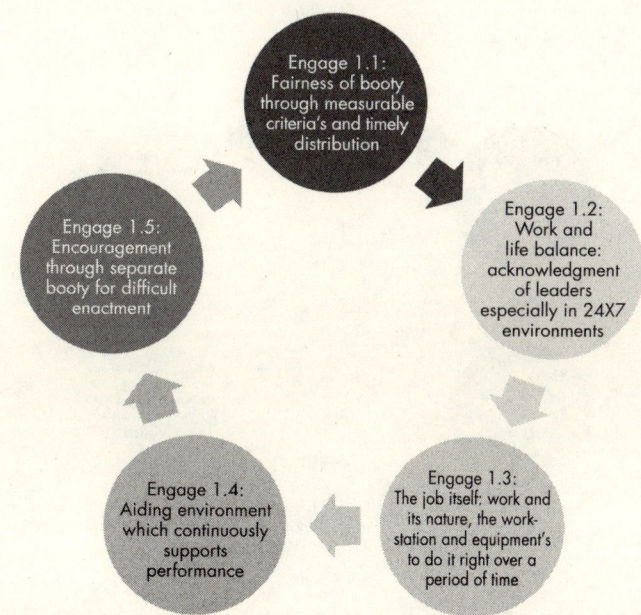

FIGURE 5.8   Factors that attract the right talent or people

Engage #2 Factors that support the system in retention or keeping the right talent.

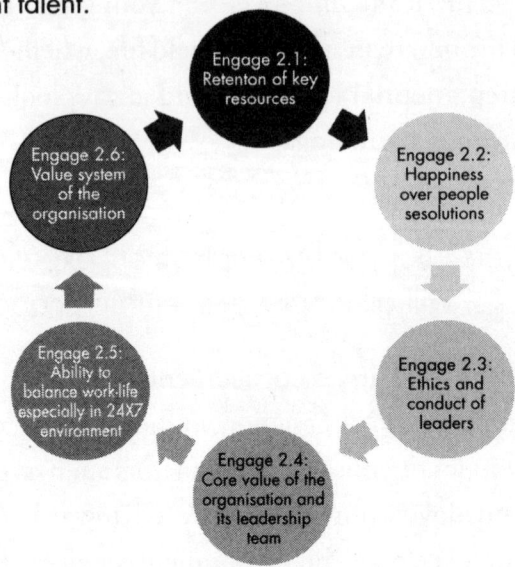

FIGURE 5.9 Factors that support the system in retention or keeping the right talent

Engage #3 Factors that support long-term engaging of key resources in an organisation.

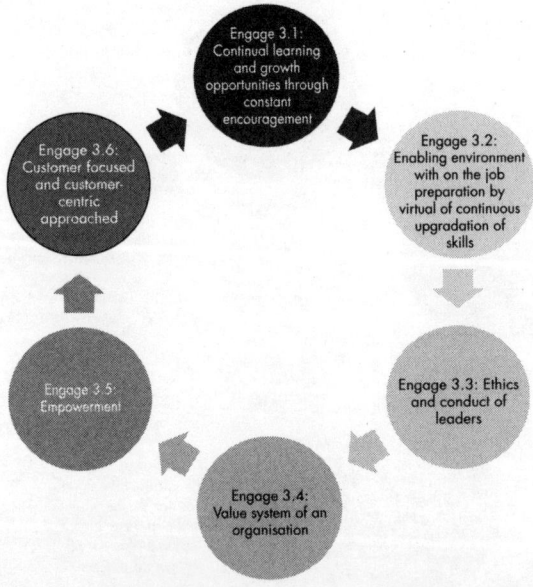

FIGURE 5.10 Factors that support long-term engaging of key resources in an organisation

5.5 Measuring how to 'keep them engaged'?

'Keeping them engaged' is a continuous process of entrepreneurial leadership, which is a universal procedure, generated out of sensitivity and thoughtfulness, rather than an irregular association.

This measure defines engagement as 'a positive, fulfilling, work-related state of mind, which is characterised by drive, guarantee, and passion for success.'

'Drive is the readiness (skill multiplied by will) to devote energy and passion in one's work and spirit, even in the face of adversity. It is branded by high levels of energy and flexibility, while performing a job.'

'Guarantee (commitment) refers to being passionately involved in job, and experience a sense of meaning, passion, energy, motivation, and pride.'

'Passion is perceived as being fully occupied in one's job, where time and work cannot be separated. It is when we willingly and happily concentrate, and are not forced to concentrate in work.'

Leaders know that engagement is a measurable construct, comparable with global/country/age-specific data. There are numerous employee attitude surveys in use currently, many developed in-house by organisations with the aim of measuring engagement levels in the company. There are also a number of measures produced by large consultancies and survey houses, which allow organisations to benchmark their levels of engagement against data derived from hundreds or thousands of companies. Then you also have experts like *Gallup*, who can give you industry specific/country specific/world data. There is no dearth of it.

5.6 Variations in how to 'keep them engaged'

Leaders are interested in the factors that affect employee engagement in part because they want to identify steps they might be able to take to support higher levels of engagements.

Taking a clue from the book 'one minute manager', we would not even spend a minute discussing old theories or existing measures. We are here to look for the new innovative measures, and we will spend each minute on it.

5.7 What it takes to 'keep them engaged'?

A people's leader should look at the information in Fig 5.11, and understand that employee engagement could hang on a range of workplace factors that are present at work, as well as characteristics that employees carry to work.

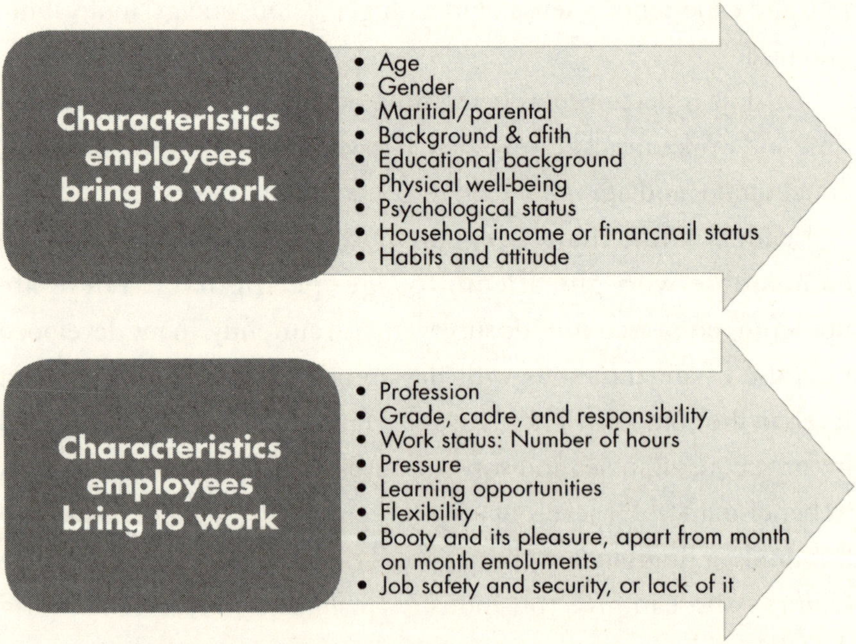

Characteristics employees bring to work

- Age
- Gender
- Maritial/parental
- Background & afith
- Educational background
- Physical well-being
- Psychological status
- Household income or financnail status
- Habits and attitude

Characteristics employees bring to work

- Profession
- Grade, cadre, and responsibility
- Work status: Number of hours
- Pressure
- Learning opportunities
- Flexibility
- Booty and its pleasure, apart from month on month emoluments
- Job safety and security, or lack of it

FIGURE 5.11   What it takes to 'keep them engaged'?

5.8 Brief steps to 'keep them engaged'

Why I have said brief is because, we need to discuss this in detail subsequently. Till then, let's list down the steps, and keep our questions to ourselves, till we complete reading the other sections.

Engage #1   Define what engagement means to your administration and leadership teams?

Engage #2   Define 'ideal worker' for your setup.

Engage #3   As a leader, define the strategy and conduct an engagement audit.

Engage #4   Look for a consequent field force analysis, if required.

Engage #5   Identify key agonising areas, and also where your organisation is not doing well.

Engage #6   Safeguard engagement action plan is made for enlightening the grey areas, and holding the scores of top indicators.

Engage #7   Go back to it periodically.

Engage #8   Periodically conduct the next survey, and improve on findings.

As people's leader, we need to build culture-driven action plan for the next 36–48 months in a medium to large-based organisation. Please note that there is no magic which can build culture overnight. Post reading this book, you all are on your own for your departments and organisations.

5.9 Moving employees to a higher level of engagement ('keeping them engaged' and improving status-quo)

Good employees are the biggest assets for their leaders, and should therefore, bring in the greatest reward. Do you agree with me as a leader? The response would be yes, in case of three out every five.

But I am shocked that in 50 per cent of the organisations, employees are viewed as an asset to be managed, rather than as individuals, who can create the next innovation for success. Why I mentioned innovation here is simple; future of leadership, engagement, talent management, and retention, are all related to modern and innovative techniques. We as leaders need to spend quality time in innovation.

Long-term engagement starts with good communication between the leader and employees, as well as among co-workers, fostering a positive operational atmosphere.

I am a firm believer, that clear and effective communication is one of the key differentiators between a good and a great organisation.

As we speak, India's engagement score is close to 9 per cent. Isn't the data alarming for a country which is going to have one of the youngest workforce in the world? All the Indian leaders should not sleep today after reading this. The fact is sometimes very hard to digest.

My thoughts would be worth it if some of you start planning for the future of your organisations right now. I won't mind if you do not take any of my ideas, but plan for the future of the country. I am very proud to be an Indian, and did not make my passport till I started visiting new countries every year to broaden my horizon. If you use my thoughts, I would definitely be a proud father and would appreciate it.

Be the market leader and not a follower or challenger. Be the first one to change. I promise, that the organisational leader, who gives me the first call post reading this, would get full support in implementing my thoughts free of cost.

An entrepreneurial leader can create positive self-esteem in team members by setting clear career paths. They need to set SMART (Specific, Measurable, Attainable, Reasonable, and Time-bound) goals, with a potential for growth year on year. It is important for each one of you to show the value for a team member. How will you do that? As a leader, you need to recognise and reward them timely, whenever they do their job well.

It is proven time and again, that we don't work for money, but for involvement. There are so many developers who work part time for the passion of developing. There are so many professionals like me, who write, and speak in various forums, for the passion we have. Search for those signs and align the path of your team member individually with it. I feel engagement has to be individual and not one to many.

It is then much easier for you as a people's manager to turn that sense of involvement into passion, and pride in ownership, which creates the highest levels of engagement with employees. That is the base of the pyramid, and if the base is correct, you have surely built one for years.

You as an entrepreneurial leader do not need to single out and work only with your top 10 per cent. The bell graphs and the process of differentiating is being thrown into garbage by many industry leaders, as each employee is important and should be given due diligence.

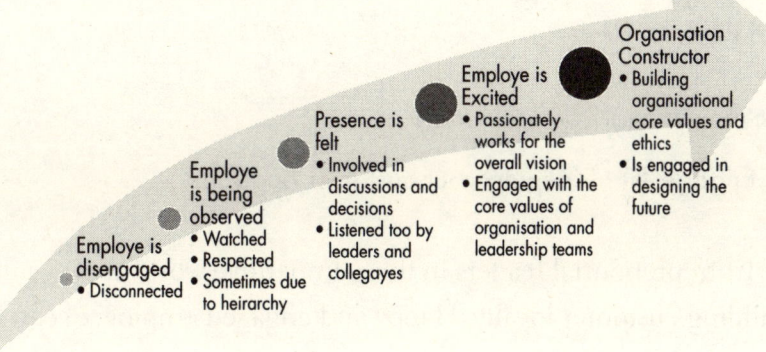

FIGURE 5.12   How to 'keep them engaged' and improve on it ?

5.10 Outcomes of 'keeping them engaged': organisational and employee level

> In a movie, a positive work of art depends on the delivery and involvement of each member of the crew. Even one of the missing links would be highlighted on the 70 mm screen. No matter how technologically advanced we are, we can still easily catch the loopholes in the movie. I am so fond of watching theatre. How many of you have watched a live one? Oh! It is such a difficult job. Just go and see one theatre in silence, and observe the artists. They can't even make a single error.

Similarly, work commitment is an involvement in itself. Entrepreneurial leaders should realise that it can be measured by reduced costs of recruitment and increase in employee output, therefore, increasing indirect productivity or positive numbers on a balance sheet.

As people leaders, by now you would have realised that improving engagement, can lead to many positive outcomes. There is a lot of literature available on it. There can be two levels of benefits: at an organisational level, and at an individual level. Let us, as entrepreneurial leaders, try and explore the current thinking on the above two, in terms of employee engagement, in the next few paragraphs.

Organisational-level outcomes

Engage #1 'Keeping your customer engaged'.

Entrepreneurial leaders in this competitive world are in game for building customer loyalty. Happy and engaged employees can build customer base for an organisation. An organisation bleeds when even one customer goes to its competitor. Along with him, s/he takes nine more at an average. Thus, it reduces the overall customer base.

65 per cent of business generated in most industries, is through reference or repeat business. An engaged employee would know more about the products, services, and organisation, and would passionately take it forward. As a result, one builds a more happy and satisfied customer base. Customer loyalty increases, therefore, towards the organisation.

The term called 'customer engagement' is defined as an emotional and demonstrative connect between the organisation and customers. You would also see in your life or must have experienced it yourself, that we do not change a few service providers, even when we change our location.

> Let us look at some of the very basic customer service examples. We are attached to an individual when it concerns service.
>
> For example, a beauty parlour or a barber, ladies or gents tailor, etc., are very simple examples of the same. The customer engagement is because of the tailor or the beautician and his/her services.
>
> Some of you would have also liked me to add a doctor to this. Isn't it? But sometimes I have seen people going to a fresh and more learned doctor who is recently educated, and who understands new medicines and theories. So I have kept this service in the safe zone.

Have you ever been a part of a customer engagement survey? Brand loyalty, resulting in repeat business, and improved profit lines, are impacted by customer engagement directly.

One interesting thing we found out in two surveys (one in a call centre, and another in a consumer durable industry), are that, a customer needs resolution timely, and all the other things like fancy words, beautiful voice, three times thank you, etc., are immaterial.

After the customer engagement survey findings in one of the world-renowned call centres, we as an organisation, learned and changed our outlook. If the agent was unable to provide solution, then it was considered as an elementary error, even if the agent had 100 per cent scores in other parameters. The agent's quality score straight-away dipped to a 'zero' for that call. The result was abnormal, and our closure rates and resolutions increased.

We could also, at a later stage, build a technical help desk, and even close some of the technical calls over the phone, with the combo of an agent and a technician. We could take customer service to the next level.

Customer engagement is completely dependent on MOT (Moments of Truth). If you do not map your delivery with the expectations, it would become negative, and on the other hand, it can also be positive or neutral. MOT is part of any interaction from advertisement, to after-sales service. There was another interesting fact which we realised as leaders, while doing these surveys, that a happy customer would be instrumental in repeat business and positive word of mouth. You as a leaders should work on creating a wow factor.

60

Engage #2   What is the output of 'keeping them engaged'?

People leaders realise that engaged employees work harder for the achievement of their goals. Employees also are more loyal, and are more likely to give an extra effort for the organisation, when needed.

A study of 50,000 employees found that the most engaged and committed perform 20 per cent better than their colleagues (Corporate leadership council, 2004). Entrepreneurial leaders should read it again, and make a note of it.

Through survey of employees, we find that the higher levels of engagement at work, support employees in taking initiative, and pursuing their learning goals.

Likewise, Watson Wyatt's survey of 946 companies across 22 countries found that employees who are highly engaged, are more than twice as likely to be top performers. This is a direct co-relation, and entrepreneurial leaders should keep a tab on it.

Employees who are engaged often present the leaders with ideas. Involvement is directly proportionate to performance, which can be easily evaluated and calculated through bottom line or productivity.

Engage #3   Would 'keeping them engaged' be self-beneficial for the organisation?

Entrepreneurial leaders should understand that engaged team members would more likely talk about the organisation positively. They may also promote its products and services personally.

People leaders should be careful of extreme negative side-effects too. It is certain that disengaged individuals would discourage others from joining their current organisation. These individuals can be termed as 'corporate terrorists'. They may also spread wrong messages, which may hurt the organisation.

It is very important, for we all live in an age where news can spread more quickly than fire. It is estimated that one negative feedback or MOT reaches 81 people, and in case of positive, only to five. The decision lays with entrepreneurial leaders, as to which way they would lead their organisations and their biggest assets, 'good people'.

Engage #4   How to keep them or retain them?

Entrepreneurial leaders are aware now, that engaged team members are certainly going to slog it out with them. It was found out that more than 80 per cent of engaged employees plan on working with the organisation, compared to about 25 per cent of disengaged employees. In addition, more than 40 per cent of engaged employees said that they would stay, even if the organisation is struggling to persist.

This is a very positive sign, keeping in mind most of the companies globally are bleeding. As entrepreneurial leaders, we need to look for these signs and appreciate them, as in long run, these are your trump cards.

Engage #5   Does 'keeping them engaged' directly impact the numbers and performance?

The employees on the top-end matrix of engagement were also the ones with the highest numbers in terms of delivery or results. It is established that there is a positive co-relationship between employee engagement and customer satisfaction. Engagement directly impacts productivity, revenue, and the bottom line. On the other hand, it is indirectly proportionate to employee attrition.

People's leaders, who are concerned about the outcome, should also be aware, that these relations have proven over and over again. Interestingly, increasing employee engagement can build an environment which significantly increases the probability of success.

Engage #6   How much would a leader's effectiveness matter in 'keeping them engaged'?

Leaders are always looking for team members who respond positively, demonstrate enactment, and succeed. This helps their leaders to be more effective, which in turn, increases their overall efficiency.

There is a direct correlation between efficiency and performance. The individuals with higher efficiency are more likely to contribute in problematic situations. The leaders are on a lookout for proactive team members who show sustained determination and resolute in their pursuit.

It can also be easily noticed that engaged employees are a source of encouragement for leaders and their own colleagues. People leaders feel good and efficient, leading the bunch of motivated teams. Engagement and a leader's efficiency can have a positive effect on one another.

Engage #7   'Keeping them engaged' directly impacts the number game.

> A great film does not guarantee the translation into numbers. If it does, nothing like it. It is a winning combo. Always, movies for masses and classes are different.

The charm of employee engagement is its proven links to balance sheets. It has to be measured time to time. It can be easily proven that employees are more productive, and contribute more financially to the organisation, if they feel involved in, and are devoted to, the organisation. Their head and heart should be into it.

There is also a positive relationship between engagement and balance sheet numbers through higher output, deals, customer engagement, and talent retention. Your passion is evident when you are communicating with an internal or an external customer. You communicate 93 per cent through your body language and gestures.

We found that companies with high levels of employee engagement (i.e., 70 per cent or more of staff say they are engaged) showed overall improvements of approximately close to 20 per cent. On the other hand, the organisations with low engagement levels (i.e., under 70 per cent of staff say they are not engaged) declined by approximately 35 per cent, and incurred losses.

Similarly, a study of 2,000 banks worldwide correlated, that with every 10 per cent rise in engagement levels, comes a four per cent rise in sales.

Wow! So can we say engagement is directly proportionate to productivity and bottom line? Yes, 100 per cent.

Studies suggest an increase in bottom-line profit, as a result of improved employee engagement levels. In addition, leaders should always be looking to correlate high employee engagement with increased turnover.

Organisations with growth and profit increases bring about a very engaged workforce as well. As profits go up, the potential for booty rises. This rubs positively with the employees, and is evident in work and its results.

You would have seen that the same actor and the same director don't produce the 'magic' on the screen. If you look at yourself, you do not produce the same results every day. Sometimes, there are days when you can't do anything right. It happens with everyone.

A leader needs to determine the results, so it is necessary to measure an engagement score over a period of time, and compare the changes during this period. Action planning and correction can only happen with sustained action, especially in the current diverse workforces.

Engage #8 Will 'keeping them engaged' help support the culture of change, especially in this dynamic market situation?

Employee engagement plays a key role in aiding the successful implementation of organisational change. It may be useful for an entrepreneurial leader, as the fluctuating dynamic market is constant in the current world. It would be important for enabling organisational nimbleness.

People are receptive to change, unless they suggest it themselves. It is sometimes important when presenting new policies and implementing change. Engagement may protect an organisation's bottom line, even when the economy is in the midst of a slowdown.

In this change, people need to constantly take decisions. This is challenging, as sometimes, even leaders do not know the path ahead. Are you facing a similar situation? Believe in yourselves, communicate, enroll them, and make them sympathetic towards change. The overall outlook has to change in this modern world.

Employee-level outcomes

Engage #1 What effects positive fitness and happiness has on 'keeping them engaged'?

Entrepreneurs may note that engagement may result in positive health fitness and positive feelings of happiness towards work and the organisation. More than 60 per cent of engaged employees report positive fitness, and they are happy to be there. Is this an indicator for us? It directly proves the co-relation between the two.

An employee is always looking for energetic and vibrant organisation to work with. Even in tough times, these employees are more likely to support you. An overall positive employee will view the job as a decent opportunity, and the environment as healthy.

Entrepreneurial leaders are fully aware that, one's work leads to core passion, positive intent, honest authenticity, open and two-way-communication, sparkle energy, ethical behaviour, determination, and participation. This results in an overall integrated and happy employee. This is what leaders of future need to be looking for, in the eyes, body language, and behaviour of employees.

Engage #2 'Matching the expectations' of the engaged employee in a 24X7 environment.

A few generations back, it was expected that an apprentice would retire from the same organisation. They expected to be recognised and promoted for the exchange of their loyalty. Now the value and the bond between entrepreneurial leaders and employees have changed.

On one side, the expectation of an employee has gone up, but on the other side, the mind-set of our customers has also changed. Customers want 24X7 service. You are expected day in and out to be available, and even in the middle of night, provide them with a solution.

It is a catch 22 situation, looking at it from an entrepreneurial angle. What choice does it leave for organisations or leaders? They will pay you more and engage you in services, 24X7.

What about employees work-life balance? It goes for a toss, doesn't it! No one is bothered about it till the arrangements work.

I know many employees, especially at the leadership or higher middle management levels, questioning the overall work-life balance and contentment. It is frustrating for many highly energetic people. If an organisation has provided you with a mobile and a SIM, it expects you to answer every call, even in the middle of the night. It won't be wrong to assess that most of you would be online, even at 12 in the night. I have been observing this trend over a long time now. All my social networking and other messages are received mostly after a normal person is in his dreams.

The days are gone when my wife used to switch off the television at 10 pm, and my kids used to sleep early. Now my 15 years old son is on his android phone and comparing notes on WhatsApp even after 10 pm. Are you into it? Technology is great, and innovation is the medium to grow, but let's not become slaves of it. We as leaders can use technology to engage. We should be able to leverage this into our benefit.

I am proud to have worked with some great leaders, and have taken so many initiatives with them.

I want to speak about something very specific though, and keep it as simple as possible. Once, while working for a consumer durable giant, we had a customer service wing, and an interface back-end software, which was accessed by 2200 service engineers across the country. Everyone had to log on to it.

We built an interface between our company's Twitter account, and this service software. So, when we used to get a customer or internal appreciation through any means, we used to appreciate the employee through 140 characters on Twitter. These characters flashed on the screens of these 2200 engineers.

What an amazing and simple innovation and out-of-the-box thinking! The numbers hit in the innovative method was the most important differentiator for the success of the initiative.

Indeed! Entrepreneurial leaders should note that an increase in an employee's intelligence, passion, and self-belief leads to an upshot of employee engagement scores. The organisations and people leaders seek this amalgamation with a pinch of positive behaviour in testing times.

5.11 Conclusion from the research

My experience and overall exposure of the research proved that engagement and productivity are directly co-related to each other. Faster the entrepreneurial leaders realise it, better they would be. It has both, direct and indirect implications on the balance sheet, and in tough times, retention of key resources.

Also, we together need to start the movement. We are at 50 per cent in terms of organisations having concrete engagement and talent management plans. It is a must to ensure that we are moving towards the right path. We need more entrepreneurial leaders to join hands with us, and invest time and energy on it.

Job satisfaction improves engagement and performance; though, we had discussed earlier that it is not mandatory that every happy and satisfied employee is engaged.

To give a great performance, an actor needs to defy all odds, come out of his/her comfort zone, and play the role of the character. They also play different shades of the character in a single day. Don't you think it requires a lot of effort?

A perfect leader has to similarly play different roles to manage different situations, thus, retaining their good employees.

Key Learnings

Performance either makes or breaks an organisation, especially in testing times. As a people's leader, you need to evaluate who would fit in your organisation, what will it take for a good team member to stick with the organisation, and how would they like to be treated. Last but not the least, what would be best for both, the team member and the organisation. Engaged people produce better results, even in companies providing the same set of service or product solutions.

Engagement directly depends on the value system of the organisation. Its superiority in relationship to the competition, opportunities to learn and grow, aiding environment which continually supports performance, work and life balance, and attainable booty month on month are directly correlated. Engagement is a positive fulfilling work-related state of mind that is characterised by drive, guarantee, and passion for success. More than 60 per cent of engaged employees report positive fitness and they are happy to be there.

Factors that attract the right talent were found as fairness of booty through measurable criteria and timely distribution, work and life balance, the job itself, aiding environment, and encouragement through separate booty for difficult enactment. Factors that we need to work on as people leaders to ensure retention of our key employees were people resolutions, ethics and conduct of leaders, core values of the organisation and the leadership team, and work and life balance, especially in a 24X7 environment.

CHAPTER 6

Belief Affirmed Through Research – 'Match the Age' to 'Keep them Engaged'

Key Objectives

- My belief, backed by positive indicators (research backed by my thoughts on 'match the age' to 'keep them engaged').
- 'Matching the age': Challenging the status-quo.
- Top 10 contributors for 'keeping them engaged'.
- 'Matching the age': Matching the percentage of respondents.
- Analysis and interpretation of key findings.
- 'Match the age': 'Keeping them engaged' v/s 'keep them satisfied'.
- Top five findings which are highlighted, and their impacts on leadership teams.

6.1 My belief: 'match the age' to 'keep them engaged'

Over the back of my mind, my belief was growing stronger and stronger in terms of different needs for different age groups. It started taking some sort of shape, post my secondary research; but its original shape came into existence post my primary research, backed by data across the globe, and India in particular. This became part of my award-winning thesis, and forced me to pen down my overall 20 years of man management experience in black and white.

6.2 My credence

Just like the film industry, no two actors can fill a single role. Every script is evaluated on who can do justice to the roles best. Everyone wants profits and wants to make a blockbuster (₹100+ crore movie). But does success comes to everyone? The answer would be no.

I was reading somewhere about, when a producer had to sign three heroines opposite three famous heroes in a multi-caster. He said to one of them, 'you are opposite the most romantic man'; to the second one, 'you are opposite the most talented one'; and to the third one he said, 'you are opposite the most handsome one and a crowd puller'. Wow! What a way to convince three top heroines to occupy only 10 minutes of screen space each.

6.3 'Matching the age': Challenging the status-quo

Leaders would have come across or followed engagement theories till date, which promulgated that, at an organisational level, there should be a single fit to all engagement plans, which is applicable commonly to each and every employee of the organisation. This is irrespective of age or sex or department, or needs. Time has come when we need to look beyond it, and look at 'matching the age'. If we don't do this now, then it would be too late.

As people managers, we need to first take a stock of the overall atmosphere in which these generations are born and brought up. We need to understand the overall culture, core beliefs, and values, instilled by us in them (as we are their parents), technological and political events in the country, and the world at large. We can walk their talk only when we understand the above. The results are – higher team engagement and sales, or improved upshot results and employee retention. In my limited submission, this is what we need. Do we need more?

In any organisation there lies a generation gap, which generates drastic difference in the outlook of employees. 'Match the age' would become a double-edged engagement and retention tool. Why I say so? People leaders and academicians would be handling in near future this outburst of Gen Y and one-click generation. 'Match the age' would help each one of them to keep their students and teams fully engaged. The book would also discuss engagement techniques, which can be easily implemented in one's life.

I had seen difference in enthusiasm towards some activities by one age group, and not so much for the other. People leaders should have also noticed the same. Hereby, thoughts were planted in my grey matter, which told me that something has to be looked at differently. I also realised, when I worked closely with people that, their behaviour and needs also changed with age or responsibilities back home. If they were looking for more benefits, they definitely would be more interested in family needs and engagement of families. We can't overlook that.

It was evident that leaders were ignoring and not recognising the difference. Maybe they thought the engagement interventions would become more complex, if they worked on the obvious difference. But ignoring the above is no solution.

As leaders, quicker we acknowledge the facts; we would be in a better position to handle it. Do all of you agree me with on this?

This was the start of my studies for obtaining a doctorate in management studies. The seed implanted blossomed into a plant, when I saw the results of the primary data through my surveys.

6.4 Top 10 contributors to 'keeping them engaged' – 'keep them engaged' v/s 'keep them satisfied'

6.4.1 Satisfaction Index Ranking

Satisfaction #1   Safety of the job itself.

Satisfaction #2   Aiding environment which continually supports performance.

Satisfaction #3   Commercial steadiness of an organisation, and the organisation's superiority in relation to the competition.

Satisfaction #4   Immediate supervisor and rapport with him/her.

Satisfaction #5   Good remuneration and safety of income in the current market.

Satisfaction #6   Fairness of booty, and benefits through measurable criteria only, and timely distribution.

Satisfaction #7   Contribution of work towards the organisation's bottom line.

Satisfaction #8   The work itself (is close to their hearts) and its nature.

Satisfaction #9   Empowerment.

Satisfaction #10   Core of the organisation and the leadership team.

6.4.2 Engagement Index Ranking

Engage #1   The work itself (is close to their hearts) and its nature.

Engage #2   Core of the organisation and the leadership team.

Engage #3   Aiding environment which continually supports performance.

Engage #4   Immediate supervisor and rapport with him/her.

Engage #5   Contribution of work to the organisation's bottom line.

Engage #6   Empowerment.

Engage #7   Good remuneration and safety of income in the current market.

Engage #8   Fairness of booty, benefits through measurable criteria only, and timely distribution.

Engage #9   Commercial steadiness of an organisation and the organisation's superiority in relation to the competition.

Engage #10   Safety of the job itself.

It is so interesting that the ten points are not ranked the same over both the parameters. Engagement, therefore, is so different from satisfaction, but it begins with it and outgrows.

With the help of leaders, my friends, and colleagues, I designed my research around three major groups of employees, divided as following:

6.5 'Matching the age': Major bucketing

Match #1   Gen Y (up to 30 years of age).
Match #2   Gen X (31 to 45 years of age).
Match #3   Baby boomers (46 plus years of age).

Why I have taken three buckets for study instead of five or two, was to ensure that I get sufficient data representation in all buckets. I also did not want it to get complicated for my leaders. I am sure each one of you reading the book, is also with me on this. In the Asian and Indian context, and the current market position, the age groups were very suitable. Also, I had to keep in mind the feasibility and comfort of solution, cost effectiveness, and ease of its implementation.

I have also, in my book, mentioned about Match #4, Gen – 'G', the current generation. With the speed the characteristics changing, I predict Match #5 Gen 'I' to also soon come into the picture. We will talk about these two generations in the subsequent modules, clubbed under one-click generation. It would have been unfair to not mention about the next generation, and how to engage it.

The responses in my studies were received from five varied organisational setups; 1 service, 1 hospitality, 1 infrastructure, 1 manufacturing, and 1 ITES. There were close to 1000 complete responses and feedback from 72 leaders and 25 human resource heads, which form a major part of findings in the book (leaders and heads of human resources were not a part of 1000).

The facts and figures definitely opened my eyes, and my belief grew stronger, as I moved ahead with the research. We can't have a single jacket engagement intervention at an organisational level, and thus, came across a strong conclusion; we need to 'match the age'.

The only common factor which leaders can argue on is work and life balance. But you all will also second my thoughts, that with the age, the power of recording, the ability of taking risks, and most importantly, listening and taking positive feedback, becomes difficult and different. These empower employees to be engaged at their respective levels.

The current market circumstances have forced me to think out of the box, and pen a chapter about it. This may be really helpful for entrepreneurial leaders, because it has been penned down, keeping in mind the current market's volatile situation.

Let's look at what I found out from my research of these five organisations. Some of these are self-explanatory.

In India, we have a distinct advantage over the rest of the world, as our workforce in the next 8–10 years or so would be one of the youngest, or in my terminology, mostly Gen Y or below 30. It is a unique and interesting challenge. On one side of the coin, we have

74

the youngest workforce, and on the other side, we do not have a concrete plan for them. We also, as people leaders, need to note the disadvantages, as our elder workforce would hit the age of retirement. Passing on the baton, apart from making a concrete plan for the future, would be key to our organisational and our overall country's success.

In films, when an actor grows old, he moves from the role of a hero to a character artist. Similarly, we as leaders also need to find the new actor, but retain the old one, and give him roles of substance. Keep both sides of the coin happy. The other side may be helpful in mentoring and hand holding. 'Matching the age' becomes more crucial for our success in both the forms.

Let's look at a very interesting case study from customer service. It is a benchmark now to pick up the phone within three rings. Which is the company that pioneered it?

It was a company which said, if we do not pick up the phone in three rings, please disconnect the phone, you might have dialled a wrong number. It was their brand promise and they delivered. It was, ladies and gentlemen, no hotel, but a courier company known as Fed Ex. Fed Ex is to courier what Xerox is to photocopy. They picked up the parcel free from home if they did not answer the phone in three rings. Their Indian counterpart also tried it, but picked up 80 per cent of couriers free, and within three months, they realised it was not their cup of tea.

It is very easy to promise a pizza free if not delivered within 30 minutes, or no charges for the bank draft post 60 minutes of waiting. These are brand promises. It is difficult to manage the brand promise. Everyone cannot.

I urge you to visit the Marriott Hotel's website, and see their employee promise. Hat's off! Publishing it on a website is so easy, but delivering it continuously and consistently is so difficult.

Due to the changing attitudes and sensitiveness, the function of people leaders becomes more critical. As in the above example, it is important to deliver what you promise. This sets the tone. To retain and engage people in diverse workforces, it is important to work on individual group needs. There are two important issues we need to keep in mind.

Firstly, the cost of attrition and re-hiring in these critical economic situations can impact us badly. Number two, the elder generation is required to train the new joiners, and pass them the baton. They have seen it all and know the organisation at the back of their hands.

Many entrepreneurial leaders are just interested in infusing new energy and talent in the organisation. This is important to broaden your core competencies, but not at the cost of being a divided workforce. On the other hand, some focus only on motivating season veterans who value relationships and skills accumulated over years. Ideally, leaders should satisfy, motivate, and retain young and veteran talent alike. It is important, therefore, to identify your 'ideal worker'.

The data which I took was based on close to 1000 respondents in total, and was broken down into designated age groups as shown in Figure 6.1. It shows the breakdown into 'matching the age',

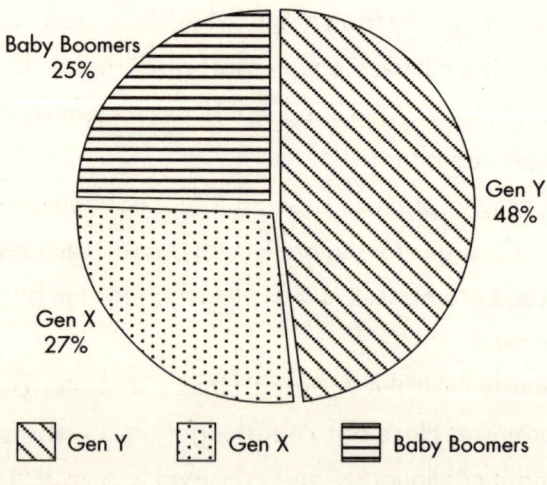

FIGURE 6.1   Percentage of respondents

i.e., three age groups of Gen Y or millennium employees, Gen X employees, and baby boomers. Gen Y or millennium employees are of the age group up to 30 years; Gen X are employees of the age group of 31 to 45 years, and baby boomers are employees of the age group of 46 years and above. One-click generation could not be represented, as this generation is still in their teens, and in school and colleges.

This is more than substantial in numbers, and I am sure has a large representation from each group. Though, I must tell you that I got only around 40 per cent full response from Gen X, 32 per cent full response from baby boomers, and more than 72 per cent full response from Gen Y. The difference in thinking can also be generated due to the above figures.

The top five key findings which were highlighted and thrown up again and again from 'matching the age' suggests that, over the course of the employee lifecycle, leaders should make note of these separately, as it would help them plan for the long term.

Match #1   For employees, the work itself (is close to their hearts), and its nature and contribution of work to organisation's bottom line, is always the principal influencer of good performance, and the utmost significant driver of retention, regardless of age. Leaders kindly pen it down. It also tells you basics first. Doesn't it?

If I am not told what my job is from Monday to Saturday, I am surely not to deliver up to your expectations.

Match #2   The core value of the organisation and leadership team becomes slightly more important in driving good performance and retention, especially in Gen Y and X. Another important point for people leaders to note is the presence of commercial steadiness of an organisation, which is somewhat related to the current economic and political turmoil.

Match #3   Good remuneration and safety of income in the current market, fairness of booty, benefits through measurable criteria only, and timely distribution of the same, are important regardless of age. It is not money which buys everything. So, as entrepreneurial leaders, we need to look at alternatives too.

Match #4   In the case of Gen Y, contribution to the society was pulled up time and again. This surprised me, but the numerous hits on the same forced me to look at the data more seriously in the chapter on Gen Y.

Match #5   Some of us, as leaders, have always believed that career concerns like title, status, prospects, and growth are very important. If you look at it carefully, it is not part of top 10 responses. It is worth noting that it becomes less important to employees as a motivator for good performance and a caterer of retention. Just for your information, out of three groups among themselves, Gen X (middle-aged supervisors/manager in India) rated this as higher than the other two generations, maybe because of family needs and social pressures.

Figure 6.2 illustrates the correlation and importance of each element in the respondent's decisions. Demands for booty and career path decreased in impact on engagement with age. As entrepreneurial leaders, therefore, we need to discuss these in depth individually.

The oldest group of respondents indicate that the work itself (is close to their hearts) and its nature, followed by commercial steadiness of an organisation, are the most important to remain with their current organisation. Overall, the image decreases slightly as a driver of retention for middle-aged respondents, compared to younger and older respondents.

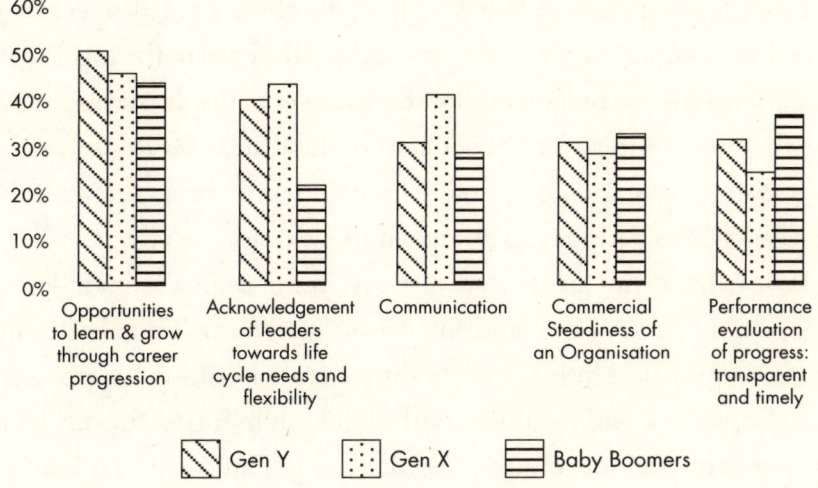

FIGURE 6.2   Elements as drivers of engagement in 'match the age '

6.6 Engagement: How does 'matching the age' works?

Engagement in very simple terms is knowing what to do at work, and wanting to do the work (knowledge/skill and attitude respectively, together establishing it into effective habits).

Knowing what to do at work includes, aligning with the vision of leaders and the organisation, and understanding how s/he can back the organisation, to achieve the vision, and be successful in the long term. The difference between a good and a great organisation is the period (long term) of success.

It is very ironical though, and please do not take me wrong when I say that, most speakers who are speaking on various forums, who have dearth of knowledge, and who have written about some of the greatest organisations, are turning insignificant. If they do not upgrade their knowledge in the current scenario, they may soon be history. Why I say so? It is simple. Out of all those organisations which they have written about, 98 per cent are non-existing in the current world. It is also advisable, therefore, to read the current and modern literature, on current organisations, practices, and human resources.

I am clearly an advocate of the thoughts of Gen Y. I also feel they have their own set career paths, especially if they are in the top 25–30 per cent league. If you don't follow their career paths, you are going to lose them to competition 90 per cent of the time. I hope you would have a fair understanding by now of how your own engagement results may vary across various age groups, if they do not already.

If you have not evaluated already, then evaluate your latest engagement survey data, and filter it by age group. The charts and figures would be close to my findings, and should open up your thought process, and would second what I am trying to convey. I am 100 per cent convinced on it, and that's why I am writing it here in black and white.

At an average, of 80 per cent (between 78 per cent and 83 per cent), individuals in all age groups, rated the work (is close to their hearts) and its nature as very important performance enablers. The company's image; commercial steadiness of an organisation; and the core values of the organisation and the leadership team; were the only elements that were rated highest by the oldest respondents (those above 46) in reference and relation to all the other age groups.

Surprisingly, good remuneration and safety of income, keeping in mind the current market trends, were rated as important by most of the Gen Y respondents.

It is important to note that this finding does not indicate that good remuneration and safety of income are less important overall in the minds of older employees, but it does indicate that good remuneration and safety of income are less effective as motivational tools for the older employees. Most of them would have, with experience, taken it for granted. Though I always feel money is secondary, and it is the satisfaction and learning opportunities which truly matter.

Generally, all indicators of rewards decrease in their potency with age. This is the second highest decline in percentage, and begins to roll-off the slide by a decade; though, the highest decline was in

80

terms of contribution of work to the organisation's bottom line as a motivator again, decade by decade.

Leaders; 'matching the age' is very similar to a leading lady in a film getting ready for a shot. The dress, accessories, and make-up, depend on the overall scheme of the plot and the film. One mistake or an error would ensure that the whole song sequence or scene goes for a toss. Definitely, we need to take or retake, think or rethink, but we as leaders can't make an error while making an engagement plan for the organisation. In movies, you get a chance to retake, but not with people as leaders.

Entrepreneurial leaders would be mostly with me till now. Yes, this part is a little boring for some of you. Please bear with me for one more minute. These are very important data, and I would love to see you all convinced post reading it. If need be, please read this chapter twice. Reading it twice will register these figures in your mind, and you would be able to correlate the same with your organisation's results. You should note to get plus/minus 3–5 per cent variance maximum in each pointer, depending on your organisation and leadership veins.

Key Learnings

Engagement needs differ in generations, mostly due to different outlook created because of our overall upbringing and culture, core beliefs and values installed in us, technological and political views in the country, and the overall world at large.

Engagement begins with satisfaction but overgrows it. For people leaders, changing attitude and sensitiveness becomes the critical driver to deliver the promise. Keeping in mind the Indian scenario, it is important that we plan and also work towards the elder generation being able to pass on the baton. Engagement in simple terms is knowing what to do at work and wanting to do the work.

CHAPTER 7

'Keep them Engaged' Across the Globe

Key Objectives

- Introduction to the current Indian and World trends, in employee engagement.
- Moving from must-have to good-to-have factors: global factors.
- 'Top half of performers' and 'bottom half of performers' based on 'matching the age'.
- Engagement differences between young and old (matching the age).

For a change, let's start this chapter differently. Let's look at couple of very interesting customer-driven examples.

LG started its beautiful campaign a few decades back, known as, 'own your own refrigerating solutions'. It was for the first time that they came up with re-stackable racks. We had till then only seen those big, iron refrigerators, where racks were fixed. The thought revolutionised the world. It became a benefit for the customer, who could literally move the rack, according to the size of the storage utensil. This revolutionary idea now has become a permanent feature.

Another interesting and different example is *ENO* and its sale in Southern India. The number of *ENO* packets sold was shocking. *ENO* was not only used there to get rid of acidity, but interestingly, it started to be used while making the batter of *idli's* and *dosa's*, which are staple in South India. What are you thinking? Even the food in Rajasthan or any dhaba in Delhi, is equally spicy, but *ENO*, for its characteristics, is used in South Indian food, thus, increasing the sale in huge numbers.

You all must have visited Northern India, and I am sure you have had a glass of *lassi*, which is a popular, traditional, yoghurt based drink from India, Bangladesh and Pakistan. Have you ever wondered, how can a small mixer grinder make 40–50 glasses of *lassi* in a couple of minutes? Is it possible! You will be amazed to find out that the ever so favourite *lassi* is made in a five kg washing machine to cater to the large numbers. Hey! Don't stop drinking it; I believe even washing machines can be used hygienically.

In 1997, when I bought that heavy weight phone from Motorola, the call rates were sky high. I even had to pay for an incoming call. It was far more feasible to disconnect the call, and call from my landline number. Today, my 10 year old daughter handles an android, and is technically far more capable then I am. My son can synchronise his mobile with a play station, and play with virtual friends. I watch them with awe.

The IBM Think Pad, which my company gave me years back to work on, is just history. New laptops and computers become absolute in every few months, because of invention in new technologies. Only human beings and their hardware are constant. You will agree that we also need to upgrade our software continuously. It stops rewiring as soon as you enter Gen X.

There are so many more examples I can list down, but what have we learnt from these examples? Two things; change is permanent, and innovation is important. Only customers can decide their own needs.

7.1 Moving from must-have to good-to-have factors 'to keep them engaged'

It is important as people leaders that we to look at the must-have factors at our work place. Until a few years back, it was easy to hold employees as they used to retire from the same organisations they started their apprenticeship from. With the advent of technology and difference in the thought process of Gen Y and Gen X to an extent, these factors have been modified. Interestingly these factors would change over a period of time with future generations.

Although entrepreneurial leaders would agree with me, that we need to definitely have must-have factors; we should also start moving towards good-to-have factors to 'keep them engaged' in the current generation. As leaders, we must also acknowledge that negative

84

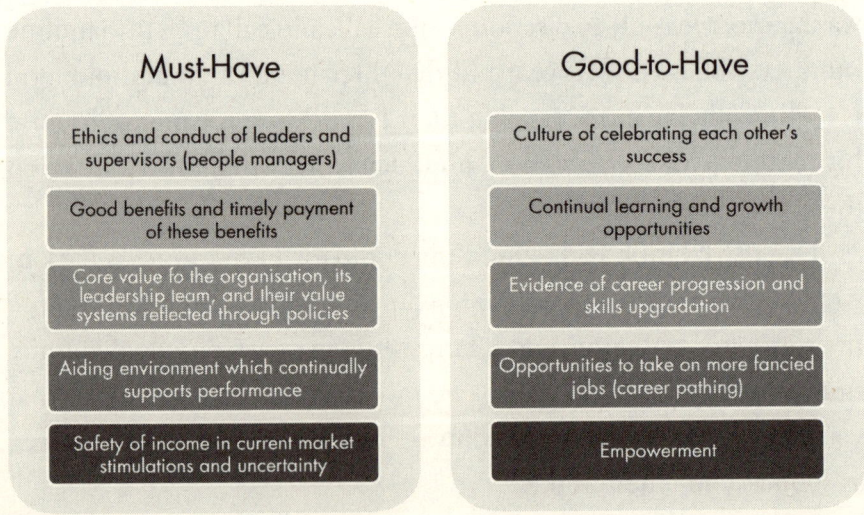

FIGURE 7.1 Must-have v/s good-to-have factors

reactions would be incurred if the must-have needs are missing, or are present in a distorted form.

7.2 Action planning

The right intent with transparency is what we need from entrepreneurial leaders. In some organisation prior to this, I have worked on zero budgets. Zero budgets never hindered my progress. Even with these constraints, our leadership team designed and conducted a survey with the help of a free website like surveymonkey.com and few others. The only point to be kept in mind was that, the survey should be an autonomous one.

There must be a buy-in from the business, and business leaders investing time and efforts in it. This would be a sure shot way to bring in success. Forced engagement action planning does not work. It is better not to conduct it.

You know your organisation best as a leader. You also know the constraints of your organisation. It is not necessary to do a fancy survey and invest in it, if your budget is limited. With a little thinking, innovation, and knowledge, you can conduct the same. Whatever method you employ, it just has to be sincere and honest.

The method of conducting is very simple. Break it by needs of age, make an action plan, and implement it. Leaders will second me when I say, every positive intent would have a positive outcome.

Let me give all leaders an interesting tip. I suggest, you should build questionnaires, starting with 'what's in it for me', and gradually shifts towards 'what's in it for the organisation as a whole'. Just follow this path and put in your efforts, because after all, it is your organisation. Every organisation differs in terms of core values and vision.

When leaders motivate their teams to perform beyond the basic duties, it definitely has to deal with high level of satisfaction and engagement. Business outcomes and bottom line results follow suit.

7.3 What is happening across the globe to 'keep them engaged'?

Each cycle of new employees may have different wants and needs, as their generation adapts to our ever-changing world. At regular intervals, entrepreneurial leaders have to reinvent the current plan for cadre building at an organisational level.

When we started our career about two decades from now, we were quite different to what we see in the current generation. Trust me, this new thought process will fade away with new ideas in a few years from now. This is a constant cycle of change. In a nutshell, we can confidently conclude, change will continue occurring, in terms of wants and needs. Technology has broken all barriers, and has ensured that we are aligned. With the expansion of business, every team leader needs to plan for the future. A well chalked-out plan will always help you to become a good leader. Keeping in mind the future, we should always work on cadre building at an organisational level.

Satisfaction is directly related to engagement of a team member and what one wants. It is always easier for entrepreneurial leaders to measure the impact. The difference between who is 'keeping them engaged' and who is 'not keeping them engaged', can easily be found if we compare two sets of organisations.

If we have to define these two sets of organisations, let us define them as 'top half of performers' and 'bottom half of performers'. The criteria which I took here was not only performance on financial matrix, but also on good talent retention over a period of time. Being a human resource head, I need to measure both.

The findings were simple; 'top half of performers' were clocking nearly double the profits, as compared to the 'bottom half of performers', even taking into account the economic crisis. The difference lies between who is 'keeping them engaged' and who is 'not keeping them engaged'.

I want all the leaders reading this book to understand the difference and ensure that your bosses should agree to this concept.

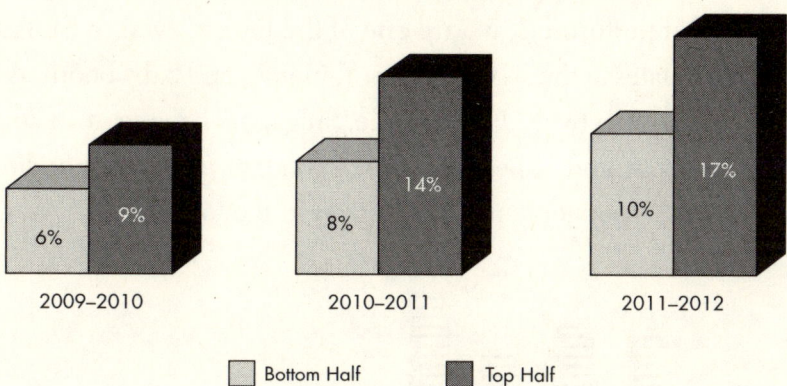

'Top half of performers' and 'bottom half of performers'

2009–2010: 6%, 9%
2010–2011: 8%, 14%
2011–2012: 10%, 17%

Bottom Half   Top Half

FIGURE 7.2   Growth in profits ('top half of performers' and 'bottom half of performers ')

The Figure 7.2 is self-explanatory, though if you take global clues, the movement of 9 per cent for 16 per cent was evident in 2011 itself.

Let us take the example of India and China, and compare their age pyramids. My main focus in these two major emerging markets is on Gen Y, those below 30 years of age. They would be one of the largest workforce populations in both the countries. Google gives you the right age pyramid or demographic figures.

It would definitely be a big plus for leaders as well as academicians, who deal with Gen Y day in and out.

7.4 Patterns: 'Match the age'

We have already highlighted the gap between the 'top half of performers' and the 'bottom half of performers' in terms of numbers. In simple leadership terms, 'top half means keeping them engaged', and 'bottom half means not keeping them engaged'.

In India, we see an interesting difference in engagement score, and it correlates with the difference in growth numbers over the years. As the employee age is increasing, the score increases, but with a dip in the middle of employee's life. If you can get hold of figures of the world, and then compare them with Indian scores, you will find that in top half of performers, we are one of the lowest, even in SE Asia.

Fig 7.3 relates to the scores of Gen Y, Gen X, and baby boomers for all countries respectively. For example, Singapore has a score of 76 per cent, 54 per cent, and 70 per cent in the lower half, and correspondingly 96 per cent, 90 per cent, and 94 per cent in the top half.

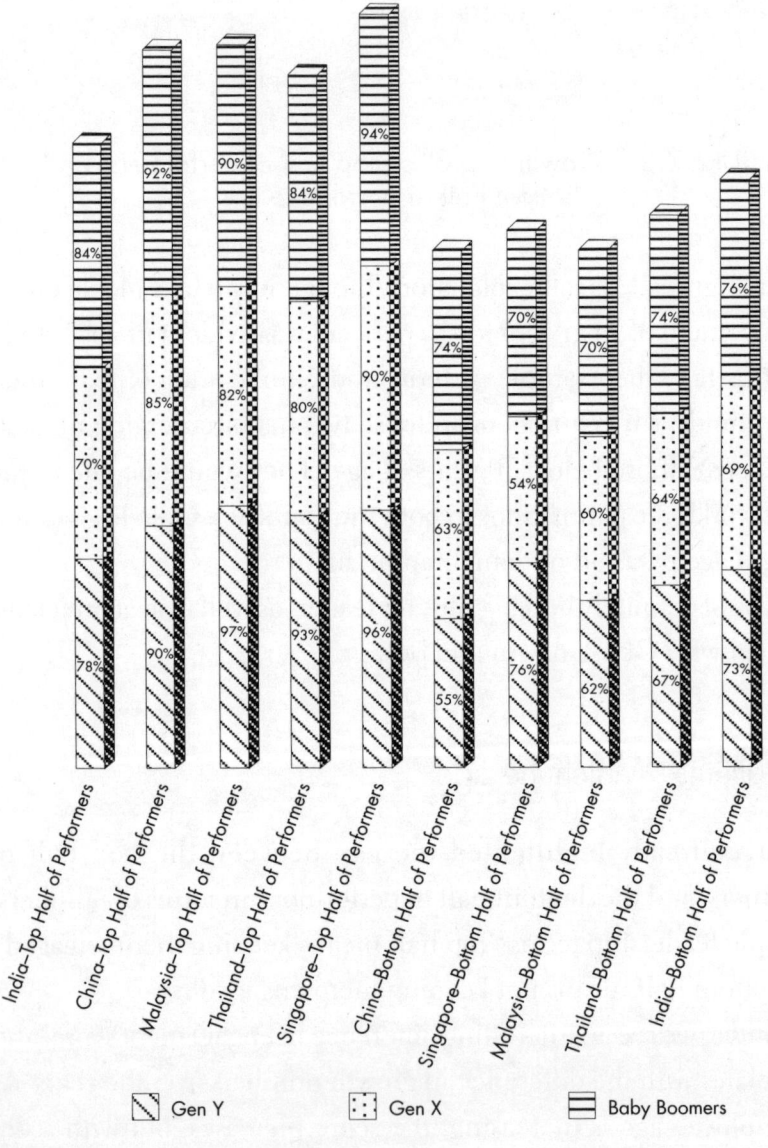

FIGURE 7.3   Relates to the scores of Gen Y, Gen X, and Baby Boomers

Similarly, if we look at the engagement scores of China, the bottom half would be 55 per cent, 63 per cent, and 74 per cent respectively, but for the top half, it grows significantly high to 90 per cent, 85 per cent, and 92 per cent. Malaysia, on the other hand, has the top end scores at 97 per cent, 82 per cent, and 90 per cent respectively. Thailand has a top half score of 93 per cent, 80 per cent, and 84 per cent.

7.5 Difference in 'keeping them engaged' by 'matching the age'

Entrepreneurial leaders need to realise that the concerns and the needs of employees vary with age. The overall concern would be the measurable, attainable, and fair booty. With the current situation, the timely distribution of the benefits becomes the most important driver. It is also surprising that booty was rated as one of the bottom three scores by most of the employees. This proves once again that money is not everything.

The 'measurable and attainable booty, month on month', were given lowest scores by the youngest generation. In the open questions though, they definitely mentioned that they get disengaged if they are not given continued opportunities of learning and growth. They need specific attention from leaders for these specific needs.

The middle-age groups (Gen X) showed a common concern for booty. They were more concerned with the increase of responsibilities in life. They would love to have flexible options, and as a leader, I feel the choice has to be theirs, as it is their hard-earned booty. This is the age group where you have a family to support and instalments to be paid. Special attention should be given to this age group by compensation experts.

The most critical in terms of view on policy was the elder lot. They were not concerned with the emoluments. Interestingly, these patterns were repeated across the region, and what fluctuated was the degree of the destructive judgement.

To 'keep them engaged', Gen Y listed their needs as good emoluments, good benefits, and timely payment; fair, measurable, and attainable timely payment of booty. They also mentioned that if they are individually taken care off, they rarely think of leaving the organisation. In certain cases, we found that within nine months, a fresh graduate tries venturing around for a job change.

Gen X, as discussed earlier, prioritised family needs throughout the APAC region. Baby boomers stated their needs, as opportunities of assuming, larger or meaty roles, and timely professional evaluation of progress. They also loved the entrepreneurship prospects through leaders and culture at an organisational level.

Worth noting is that 55 per cent responses from Gen Y indicated that they are unique and they need specific and different strategies to be engaged. Do you agree with them? I surely do.

I think it is time to take a coffee break, as we head to the next important section of the book, where we look at the reasons which forced me to pen down my overall experience in form of 'match the age' to 'keep them engaged'.

In the next chapter of the book, we look at taking the concept of 'match the age' to 'keep them engaged' forward, by looking at the general recommendations at an organisational level. One thing is for sure, that by now, you would have realised that motivators are different for different age groups, and so are the corresponding engagement needs.

Key Learnings

In these testing times, it is very difficult to attract the right talent. It is necessary that we induce ethics and values for leaders and supervisors. We provide good benefits and their timely payments to enhance the same. These are reflected through policies and are important for attracting right talent, especially through referrals.

Aiding environment and stability of the organisation would ensure safety of the income, which is very important in the current scenario. The value proposition for an employee may come from opportunities to take on larger roles, evidence of career progression, skills upgradation, continual opportunities to learn and grow, and culture of celebrating each other's success. These few are also differentiators in terms of employee engagement and retention. Top half of the performing companies produced nearly double the profit compared to the bottom half, even in these economic crises.

Most importantly, keeping in mind our future, people leaders should take note when more than 55 per cent of younger generation indicates that they are unique and need specific, individual strategies, to be engaged.

CHAPTER 8

General Recommendations for 'Keeping them Engaged'

Key Objectives

- Taking a step forward from the study and looking deeply at the concept of 'keeping them engaged'.
- Leaders should recognise the importance of 'matching the age'.
- What is the definition of 'ideal workers' in your organisation?
- Define what 'keeps them engaged' in your organisation.
- Conducting an organisational audit.
- Identifying the action steps.
- Factors which 'keep them engaged' and boost performance.

In the last learning module, we have discussed in depth various permutations and combinations of employee engagement statistics. Moving forward from there, let's look at what would help us and our teams, and thereon, work on a general action plan on engagement.

8.1 Taking clue from the study and looking deeply at the concept of 'keeping them engaged' for long periods in an organisation

Let's recapitulate and re-evaluate the top 12 points, which should be at the back of our hands. If possible, read them over at least twice to ensure that we are on the same page. These should haunt you hereon, till you do not put them into concrete actionable solutions.

Engage #1   Firstly, leaders would be required to think differently, and with open mind towards the innovative concept of 'matching the age'

Engage #2   Like me, I am sure there are many of you who believe that the younger generation is splendid and should be given right opportunities. Keeping this in mind, we need to pass on the skills and knowledge. It is important for us to keep our workforce diverse, with the right mix, towards our definition of an 'ideal employee'. Energy and spirits go hand in hand. Overall, younger generations have lower engagement scores, and we need to constantly work on it.

Engage #3   Safety of the job itself; commercial steadiness of an organisation; the organisation's superiority in relation to the competition; and the core values of the organisation and the leadership team, are the important factors listed. They have direct impact on the physical and mental health of an employee. Entrepreneurial leaders should note that team members with better physical and mental health are likely to have higher levels of engagement, than those with poor physical and mental health.

Engage #4   Leaders would have also noted that continuous opportunities to learn and grow through career progression ensures higher levels of engagement, than those who are not satisfied with them. Irrespective of age, employees stay with the organisation for the learning opportunities. Good leaders do not ignore this, and therefore, great companies have it in their scheme of vision itself.

One of the extremely alarming facts that the data throws out is that leaders deem talent engagement and retention as important. Most of the organisations do not have a concrete plant to tackle it.

The companies that do not have training and development in their action plan or the leaders who does not believe in the benefit of training and development, should look at the differentiators and score variation, by comparing the companies having these.

Engage #5   We all know team goals are important. When you work with companies of repute, you are always evaluated as an individual, and your contribution to the team. It should ideally comprise of 60–70 per cent of individual goals and the remaining should be team goals.

Employees working in teams have the values of being helpful, and vibrant. They are more likely to have higher levels of engagement.

I am a strong advocate of working in teams. It also ensures that you learn how to communicate, work for each other, and most importantly, defend the weakest link.

94

Let me give you a simple example. It is worth noting how an intelligent captain would hide the weakest fielder or team member from the opponent. This may be a difference between a great leaders and a good one.

Engage #6   Another interesting factor highlighted was empowerment. The organisations who did well on this same front had a concrete empowerment matrix. Empowerment enables trust between customer-organisation-employee. The front-end team members or client-facing teams need empowerment to the highest extent, to ensure that the customer is satisfied and engaged.

Allow me to share with you an interesting example of a mobile service provider. All of them provide the same product and service; however, people prefer the service of one service provider over the above.

Why? Have you ever given it a thought?

Mostly, people call up call centres when they have no time, and when they are fed up with services. Isn't it? When in trouble, you need quick resolution. For resolution, the call centre agent needs empowerment to solve your issue in most cases as soon as possible.

You get very irritated when you are kept on hold for a long. We all have faced this situation sometimes or the other, where, you are charged for the call, and are also subjected to irritating music on the other end.

What do you think is the problem? The call handler is not empowered enough to take the decision then and there, and thus, the service provider loses a valued customer.

You would see empowerment matrix very evident in sales teams. For example, if you buy a car or a house, you may be given 1 per cent discount by a sales team member and 2 per cent by a manager.

Even in tour operators, I have seen that there is empowerment of allocating the rates, based on the clientele. Have you ever thought how it would feel if the sales executive sitting right in front of you, calls the superior in regular intervals to confirm the discounts?

A simple empowerment would have reduced the hassles and improved the customer engagement. This would also help in building brand loyalty.

Engage #7   Social security is important for any employee, irrespective of age. Most of the organisations offer health and safety benefits to the employees and their families, apart from statutory benefits prescribed by the Government of India.

Entrepreneurial leaders would agree that the employees with these social security, are more likely to have higher levels of engagement.

Fortunately, I am currently working in an organisation which believes in covering employees and their parents in these schemes. We also have an extensive accidental insurance coverage. Our leaders even believe in social security for contract workers or consultants and their families. This is a step further in the right direction. For all these, there is no employee deductions.

Apart from these normal facilities, we also have funds for critical treatments. To top it all, we also have an MD's fund. When someone in critically ill and the treatment crosses his/her medical limits, the same fund can be used. Apart from this, we also have a central fund at the corporate level, which is run by an autonomous body for fatal diseases.

Another exceptional social security plan we have is the housing loan scheme, where we finance housing loans up to the prescribed limit, post five years of continuous service. We try and provide shelter for everyone.

What would be the engagement levels in the organisation? What would be an engagement level post 5 years? In the current market scenario, more social security means more engagement of the employee.

Mr Mahesh Babu, MD of IL&FS Environmental Infrastructure and Services Limited; shared his take on the above. He felt the company's vision is people centric to ensure that we make tangible difference to each and every human being around us.

We have always believed in getting mainstream environmental and social concerns into everything we do. He strongly felt that for matching the age, the time has come to preserve the environment for future generations.

I am very proud to be associated with an organisation which has always believed in working for the people and sustainability.

Engage #8 'One size does not fit all' when it comes to the steps that employers can take with regards to employee engagement. It is important to 'match the age'.

Leaders might want to focus on specific drivers of engagement for some employees in particular age/generational groups, and other drivers for some of those in other groups. It has been proved that age and maturity need to be looked at differently.

Engage #9   The attrition levels are the highest in Gen Y. Leaders need to control the same, and it may be the differentiator in the long run. I have closely observed graduate engineer trainees and management trainee, from great colleges getting disengaged in an average 6–9 months from joining. I can understand that this may be due to lack in commitment levels (what was promised at campus v/s delivery), disability to fit into the core values of the organisation or the leader, etc.

India would have one of the youngest workforce in the world in the next 8–10 years. Keeping that in mind, people leaders need to find a way to engage Gen Y effectively.

Engage #10   Access to the flexibility needed to fulfil work and family responsibilities is one factor that is associated with higher levels of engagement among Gen X employees. They also want to have flexible options and higher level of take-home salary.

Engage #11   Satisfaction with training and development is one factor that is associated with higher levels of engagement among younger generations. They come into the organisation with lot of positive and vibrant energy, and it is our job as entrepreneurial leaders to utilise that.

Engage #12   I have been conducting engagement surveys for years now. I have also worked for organisations following major international surveys like *Gallup*.

I have never seen a clearer indication on good remuneration and safety of income in the current market; fair and timely distribution of booty; and commercial steadiness of an organisation. These few were rated and explained in open questions again and again. I think it is because of the current economic and political turmoil across the globe.

Whatever be the reason, it shows a very worried working class. It also impacts their productivity directly. If we, as entrepreneurial leaders, can work with them, take extra care, be their friends, mentor them, and communicate the truth, I see teams working towards the overall organisation's growth. If they are safe and if their families are safe and involved, half of your job is done. Build emotions and strengthen your workplace. The 'magic' will be created by itself.

8.2 'Matching the age' is important: employers should recognise it

Entrepreneurial leaders should not ignore the two important challenges lying in front of them, which are the shifts in the age of majority of workforce and its diversity. We are already late.

As people leaders, we should remember that reflection of the aging population, is the aging of workforce. Their experience, and sometimes practical knowledge; the ability to connect at the same wavelength, is important for closing the sale. Sometimes, a customer can be more easily convinced by an experienced representative of an organisation. Retirement of elderly workforce could change the dynamics of an organisation, and this economic crises can be demotivating. These team members are more knowledgeable and know how to handle problems.

There are two genuine factors that an entrepreneurial leader can be concerned with. The first would be the retirement of the senior-most employees, and the second would be young workforce in surplus.

Organisations do not have enough people in Gen X (31–45) for these retiring baby boomers. Also, interestingly, Gen X is most cynical about the Gen Y. It is a catch 22 situation, and we need to 'match our knowledge' to ensure that the organisation doesn't bleed any further.

Some parts of the country may not have surplus labour. Even if you look practically around you, the workers at the factory level or the grass-root level are not available in the market.

> When I was working in a steel plant, I found it very difficult to get the number of workforce which was required.
>
> The reason is simple; the job opportunities backed by government schemes in some states, ensure that these workers do not leave their home town. After all, nobody wants to do all the hard work, leaving their families behind.

8.3 Age matters

It is important for every employee, across every generation, to love the place where they are appreciated regularly. Their alignment with the organisation and its leaders also adds value. Every team member also looks at on-the-job learning opportunities, and growing their own talent. People leaders need to ensure the above, otherwise the workforce will definitely going to be disengaged.

8.4 Which employees are considered to be 'ideal workers'?

Leaders please answer. In your set up, who is an 'ideal worker'? Does it depend on age or performance?

> If we compare it with the movie-making example discussed earlier, isn't it quite similar to finding an 'ideal actor', which suits the role perfectly? Many a times, movie projects are halted or dropped, when an actor delays or refuses a role. Similarly, as a leader, one has to pick and choose the perfect suit for the job assigned. With regular appreciation and correct remuneration, this novice becomes a future leader.

It is your vision and you as a leader need to answer these questions at this stage. Post answering all your questions, plan your engagements. I have conducted engagement surveys in five organisations, and learned that scores may be similar in a set up, but the ethos and the character of every organisation is different. Every organisation's core values are different, and therefore, their action plan should be treated in a unique way.

Entrepreneurial leaders always wish they only had 'ideal workers' in their systems. An 'ideal worker' for them is someone who is positive but aggressive, self-determined to handle adversities, single-mindedly devoted, has a balanced approach, and is not emotional.

It is similar to a father searching for a bride groom for his daughter. It is really unrealistic to ask for so many positive indicators. Leaders are looking for 'the magic'. If someone has all of these traits, then he/she should be valued as a high potential employee. Isn't it?

It is important here to discuss a very difficult issue. I have come across team members who are no more inclined in their ascent to the top. They are normally the senior citizens of your office. How do you manage them? It does not mean they wish to retire or not learn in their jobs. Leaders should note that being not interested in the overall growth does not make them exceptional or disengaged.

The other extreme prospective is very challenging. To handle the Gen X and the Gen Y, who are always keen to climb up the corporate ladder within a short term, is always challenging.

Regardless of age, people managers would love to remain the best employers or employers of choice for all employees. They would, therefore, internally have to work on the definition of 'ideal workers' in their respective set-ups. They then identify steps to take so that their young employees, middle-aged employees, and older employees, are separately motivated. Simultaneously, they attract them and keep them highly engaged in their daily work schedule, and thus, building the desire to stay with the organisation for a longer period of time.

At this juncture, I want to repeat what I had been telling to all potential leaders. It is not necessary to evaluate the performance of an employee by the time span he/she spends with the organisation. It is more important to evaluate his/her potential during the time he/she spends.

Enhancing employee engagement requires leaders to make a long-term commitment. The quick-fix approach is rarely sufficient or sustainable. Perpetual fire fighting would lead to disengagement.

I hope the following steps would help you get started as leaders and lead to 'the magic' at your workplace. Of course, organisations might decide to change the order.

As we discussed above, the definition of an 'ideal worker' would show you what you want from the employee in your organisation. What would be your overall focus and plan? It would not only depend on the maximum employees in your workforce in whichever bucket they are, also takes into account the knowledge of leaders, who have spent considerable time in the organisation. These leaders would deem the organisation as close to their hearts and would be best suited to frame an action plan in black and white.

8.5 Define what 'keeps them engaged' in your organisation?

For a leader, engagement can mean different things. Here are some pointers to keep in mind. Please remember you are the best judge and you would know what type of uniform your employees need to wear.

Engage #1   To 'keep them engaged', leaders must first learn to distinguish influencers of engagement from processes. This would enable them to list down factors for their teams and what aligns them.

Alignment may sound different to different group of individuals. Teams can be aligned with sports, CSR, or similar interest activities.

Let's take a practical example. For instance, let's assume you want to examine the relationship between engagement and individual performance. You may as well include some questions in the engagement survey for the same.

Leaders may want to know how to measure the tangible part of engagement scores. Leaders may like to measure it with their previous surveys, with the global trends, or country specific or industry-specific trends.

At this stage, people leaders need to consider whether they should develop their own measures, use a measure of employee engagement that has been used by other workplaces, or go for an external standard global benchmark. There can be advantages with each approach. Developing a customised measure will fit your needs, but has to be reliable and autonomous.

Budget is the last thing that should deter you. There are ways to conduct a free survey on a website like survey monkey. Think out of the box friends, and don't get bogged down by budget.

On the other hand, using an existing instrument or a world-renowned tool like *Gallup*, often makes it possible to compare your results, with the levels of engagement in other organisations globally.

The results have to be autonomous and protected. You cannot share results of a team of less than 10 members on any parameter. This would ensure an autonomous approach. High integrity and right intent should support you in your cause.

Even small gestures make a lot of difference. We used to send food for our trainees who were unwell from the hotel. It was such a simple, parental gesture. It had a valuable impact on our engagement scores.

Taking it a step forward, it is important for you to define, as a leader, what is your vision at the organisational level, and then plan your engagement and retention policies accordingly.

8.6 Conducting an organisational audit (to know what 'keeps them engaged')

This is the real starting point. Post planning and deliberation, leaders decide on an organisational level audit. When focussed on engagement, the audit would provide leaders with an overall sense of feelings. The employees would indicate through this survey their emotions. Leaders would have to work hard on these employee perceptions.

An employee engagement audit should emphasise the following points:

Engage#1   Assessment should measure the overall behaviour of team members in relation to circumstances. This would be a reflection of their attitude.

Engage#2   Survey should measure what employees think of factors which motivate or demotivate them.

Engage#3   Engagement survey should try and capture diverse level of workforce. It should simply give you an age wise, function wise, department wise, and role-wise activities that encourage and discourage engagement.

Engage#4   It should somehow even ask the employees how to make the change or how to make them happier and engaged. How differently would employees like to see the entrepreneurial leaders act?

If it is an internal survey, you can design your questions to measure other issues based on the overall culture, vision or values, salary and wages, intent to leave, etc., and many more.

It can definitely guide the leaders to identify areas or parts of the organisation where there are high levels of engagement. These success stories can be replicated in an organisation. When you share success stories, the buy-in from the business is quicker.

Some points to be thought and discussed again:

Match #1   The audit has to be autonomous, even if it is internal.

Match #2   It may be conducted on a website like surveymokey. com free of cost, if budgets are a concern.

Match #3   If it's an internal audit, it is fine to measure other key parameters apart from employee engagement.

Match #4   At the end of any survey, it is good to have some simple open-ended questions. Let me give you some examples; list three things we should continue in the organisation or three things we should change in our organisation.

8.7 Identify action steps (what would help you to 'keep them engaged'?)

In the Indian film industry, there are so many actors available. Some of them are exceptionally popular. They either work for classes or masses. Everyone is different in his own sense, and his reach to his specific audience is very different.

Director are very comfortable with a set of actors. They have their favourites. Still, depending on the script, they sometimes come out of the comfort zone and cast a completely different actor, most suitable for the role.

Very similarly, leaders believe in some actions and styles. Sometimes, based on the employee's feedback and perceptions, leaders need to change their style or approach. It is the demand of the script or the situation. The idea behind retention through engagement and movies is similar.

Keeping the same in mind, leaders need to look at the following 12 steps to create a concrete action plan:

Engage #1   Implementing an action plan requires a lot of courage and the ability to accept the truth. The survey is the true reflection of your organisation. The faster you accept this fact, the better you are. This would be the key differentiator between a good and a great leader.

Engage #2   Like in any pyramid, your engagement survey also caters to the basic important questions first. The corresponding action plan should always be based on a similar pyramid approach. Primarily, we work on basic questions and their action planning. Addressing the hygiene factors are important before moving to the next stage. If the engagement scores on the bottom questions are good, then we move to the next level of questions.

Engage #3   As a leader, you may want to take a number of action steps post the survey. Some organisations decide to focus on a single driver of engagement, such as supervisor support; perceptions of inclusion, and work-life balance. Others may want to adopt a more comprehensive approach, addressing several factors at one time. It completely depends on your organisation's values; the leadership team's thought process; and the availability of time and resources.

Engage #4   It is important to prioritise the action plan. Pick up first the lowest hanging fruits. They are the most fast and easy to implement, and high-impact items.

Let me give you a simple example. The key result area for all employees is easy and fastest to get results. It also caters to the bottom-most question: do I know what I am expected to do? Keeping this is mind, it is the first question that we need to tackle if scores are not good enough.

Off late, organisations like GEE or British Airways have started working on an engagement survey once in two years, instead of the yearly routine. It is difficult to impact the big ticket items in a year. It is important to decide the frequency based on your organisational needs.

Engage #5 Many leaders will be relieved to find out that it is probably not necessary to develop an engagement initiative for the sake of it. Many a times, existing programmes could just be tweaked to support increased engagement. It is not a very costly affair. It is more efforts than money, and more intent than show off, which is noticed by the younger generation of smart workers.

Engage #6 Engagement is an individual need, and differs from employee to employee and generation to generation. It is important to move it from 1 to many to a 1 to 1 approach.

Engage #7 Communicate where you are and what you intend to do? Also communicate what specific roles you want the employees to play in its success story. Always involve them and make them responsible; if they take up the ownership, half of your battle is won.

Engage #8 By now, leaders must be having a sense of their current levels of engagement. Leaders also have future levels in their minds. They implement steps for improvement and then gather data to determine the success of their efforts.

Engage #9 It is important for leaders to make a step-by-step action plan, follow it up periodically, and correct it if required.

For success of an engagement plan in the long term, it is important that all open issues are closed.

Engage #10   Action plan is always incomplete without targets and dates. They have to be attainable. Business is important. This is where the clash begins. Good people are also equal, or more important to the success of the organisation.

Engage #11   Re-conduct the internal audit or dip test of the sample population, to ascertain if you are on the right path. This is very important if we decide to conduct the engagement survey once in two years. Sample population or departments are used in the dip test, to measure the effect.

Engage #12   As a leader, it is our duty to translate this into a return of investment. I am sure all leaders, at the end of the day, want more productivity and better returns. It is important to showcase the tangible and intangible results, post an engagement survey. How has it effective, year on year? Showcase it, and look for tangible numbers or changes in matrices.

There are few very important points which come into my mind, before we hit the paddle. Let us list them down.

Engage #1   Please do not make engagement data centric. As an entrepreneurial manager, do not just get into the mode of evaluating data too much. Move ahead, make concrete action plans, and correct them on the way as you move forward.

Engage #2   As good people managers, I am sure you are close to your teams. It is important to connect with each one of them. A great leader does not need scores to reflect the mood of the teams. He/she can, in an instinct, confirm if something is wrong.

Try this: Do not speak to your team for a week. Just stay away. After a week check on their disengagement level. You will see the dip in the level of engagement. We are human beings, and we have emotional connect in any relationship.

Let me take you through innovative and current work that great organisations are doing. They are passionately innovating and doing some fabulous work on engagement. Some of them have given all their people managers, including supervisors, a tool to take a dip test, whenever they feel they need to conduct it. It is a small electronic tool, like any ordinary survey tool. The leader does not wait for an annual survey.

On the other hand, it is his/her team, and thus, the team's alignment and engagement are overall his/her responsibility. The tool ensures that he/she can take corrective actions there and then.

Why only engagement? This tool can be used in so many other ways! It can measure so many small, yet critical differentiators, very quickly.

If you look at some of the call centres, they have a mirror on the desk. It signifies that you are on stage, and you need to smile and answer all calls. Smile is felt on phone and it generates positivity.

In another interesting industry, hospitality, you have these large, full-size mirrors on the back door of the restaurant. Anyone entering into the restaurant has to erase the frowns, smile, and serve the guests. You are again onstage.

We had tried something very different and unique, when I used to work for a call centre. We equipped our team members with red and green flags. When a person was not feeling too happy or was down, he/she could raise the red flag. We knew, as their leader, that we had to sort out an issue. We used to take them off the call, and have a cup of coffee with them. Understanding and listening to them, solves 60 per cent of all problems. Solutions, if possible, were a positive team builder. We, in surprise checks, awarded the teams with maximum green flags. This also improved the team leader's performance by a notch.

You, as a leader, know your organisation the best. All the solutions mention here would have not worked in some parts of my career. Say, for example, in a steel manufacturing giant, with an average age of 45 +, these flags can backfire. So, think, and come out with a solution, which works best for your organisation.

8.8 Factors which 'keep them engaged' and boost performance

Engage #1   Work and life balance.

Work-life balance is critical, especially when we consider current customer expectation of 24X7 service.

It is important to note that we demand 24X7 service from service providers, especially in the service industry. Leaders and employers are forced to hire employees at a higher cost, but with lesser work and life balance. Leaders look for team members who are willing to sacrifice the work-life balance, and indirectly their personal life, by pushing their heart and soul into the job.

But how should a leader proceed? By offering flexi time to employees or by letting them work at home at will? Should they offer facilities like free child care, elder care, and employee concierge?

There is no one jacket answer, as it depends on the needs and basic character of your workforce. You may go for childcare, if you have a higher percentage of single parents in a call centre scenario. You may have to find a different solution for your organisation.

As per my studies, work and life balance was the major fall out and the most common factor in all generations. The scores were badly hit in most of the service companies in the Indian scenario. The younger lot were most vocal and demanding on the work and life balance. They believed in made-to-order relationships between an employer and employee, to tackle the same. It would be a very big challenge in the years to come, keeping in mind the demographics of the Indian work force.

Let us look at a real time example of *prudential life insurance*, and more importantly, learn from it. It reiterates, why it's not enough merely to offer attractive work and life benefits.

Prudential's family-friendly benefits package, which included a flexible work option, was superb, earning the company recognition in the business press.

However, an internal survey of female executives showed that 56 per cent felt that their work negatively affected their personal life. Only 45 per cent of high performing employees at the company felt that their managers support flexible work arrangements.

What is the learning for you as a leader? The learning is simple, that an action plan is not effective, unless implemented in true sense and spirit.

Engage #2   Surroundings.

Leaders, who control organisational resources, understand the intrinsic battle on the job. On one hand, the resources to create a friendly environment are limited, and the empowerment to take timely decisions is non-existent, especially in countries like India.

On the other hand, we know as leaders that work itself, and its nature; driving individual safety and well-being; tools to continually generate quality output and opportunities to learn and grow through career progression, will help improve the bottom line.

A marketing analogy would be apt here. Marketers would ideally use all available media to promote their products. But it is excessively luxurious, and they rely on market information and classy methodical tools to make strategic choices. Those with the best information and the best analysis, normally get the biggest chunk.

Leaders need to think the same way about investments, to create an enabling environment. They need to use the information available to them in the best possible way, and groom the leaders for the future.

My research has shown that most companies do not define a systematic way to determine where the real 'pain' is in relation to their workforces. They often rely on the 'squeaky-wheel-gets-the-grease' methods. You should not give in to the shrill thrill, but work on what's the best for your organisation in the long run.

In consumer marketing, this is the equivalent of making product changes, in response to feedback from early adopters, or people who call in and write letters. Chances are very high that we may miss in terms of masses, as it does not represent all consumers. It is also important to get the feedback of actual users who are also not writing in to you.

In customer service, it is important to note the hidden feelings. A customer who is complaining is better than the customer who is quietly exiting the system, without giving you an opportunity to correct yourself.

Similarly, for entrepreneurial leaders, it is important to take feedback from the larger chunk of employees. The more, the merrier. Also, on the same grounds, your interventions should also target the larger chunk of employees, and not merely 10 per cent of the population.

Our overall engagement scores are reflective. We would be lying if we say that we did not know it. It is very heartening to see people leaders not reacting to these low scores of a fully engaged population.

Globally fully engagement scores currently at 13 per cent and only 9 per cent Indian scores on the same scale, are a big disaster. Though on the other hand, it gives us an opportunity to innovate and challenge the status-quo.

People leaders need to consider how investments in employees will affect the bottom line and delivering where it matters most in an enabling yet cost-effective way.

8.9 Why then is there an overall inconsistency?

Any disconnect between company policy and a people leader's behaviour poisons employee attitudes. If we go back to the *Prudential's* example, it was simply evident. The organisation encouraged flexibility, but individual leaders didn't buy the company philosophy, and discouraged their people from taking advantage of the benefits.

Did *Prudential* learn and change anything? Yes they did. *Prudential* now trains leaders to negotiate flexitime arrangements; how well leaders do this is now one of the criteria for determining their booty.

Perception is important when considering work and life benefits. The *Prudential* experience shows that even investment in work and life benefits can deliver a negative return, if leaders send an inconsistent message with the company policy.

These examples can be found anywhere in our daily lives. It is important as people leaders that we all are on the same page before implementing these ideas.

8.10 Measurable and attainable booty month on month to 'keep them engaged'

In the Hay Group research project on rewards, several high level employees at Wall Street brokerage houses were interviewed, who had recently received half million dollar bonuses.

Several echoed the sentiment of one broker, who said, 'Getting the money was great, but it was also a bit of a let-down. What I really wanted to hear was "Thanks. You did a good job." But all my boss did was hand me a check.'

It completely re-echoes my words that booty is not everything which an employee looks for. Definitely, it can be one of the reason to be happy. On the other hand, sometimes, even a small touch or appreciation of each other can do wonders.

A letter of encouragement by email is not good enough as opposed to a handshake (or a hug for that matter). An honest pat on the back and acknowledgement increases the use of the most powerful sense, touch. Have you ever felt the power of touch?

Let me take you back to one of the very interesting experiments conducted on the power of touch. Behaviour scientists divided chimpanzees into few groups. They were allowed to use only one sense in a group. One group was allowed to touch (feel) and not use any other sense; similarly another group was allowed to speak; while the next group was allowed to only see. They were then kept like that over a period of time.

After a period of six months or so, they all were brought back to normalcy.

All the groups of chimpanzees remained the way they were, abnormal. They developed complications, except for the group with the power of touch. The group which used feel and touch as only sense, became normal over a period of time. The experiment, and its results, speaks volumes for itself.

The most powerful sense, therefore, is touch. Use it. How many times have you hugged your colleague in the last week or so? How many times did you pat their backs for a good job or suggestion? I know, they are paid for it. Believe me, just try and follow what I am saying. I am sure you will see the difference.

It would be wrong on our part if we assume that salary, incentives, and benefits, and in the current circumstances their timely distribution, are not important. But they are definitely external motivators, and rarely give employees meaning. To create 'the magic', you need to be more innovative and have positive intent. You should do more than paying just the salary.

As leaders, it is important to distinguish between performers and non-performers. Team members notice very quickly their recognition and the lack of it. Below standard recognition for hard work can be one of the most dangerous disengagement reasons for an organisation.

> I remember an incident which still brings a smile on my face. A friend of mine, CEO of a company, asked to take an exit interview of a very important employee who had put down his papers. He did not want to lose him at any cost.
>
> In the interview, we realised that he was getting less paid in the next organisation; still he wanted to leave. On drill down, we got a very funny reply from him, stating that the new workplace is walking distance from his home.
>
> It brought a smile to my face, but we genuinely could not retain him. We all are human beings and our needs are different and specific; sometimes in the best of situations, we fail. If the intent is right, failing also is a learning experience.

When it comes to measurable and attainable rewards, here are two measures which smart companies take to engage employees:

Engage #1   As leaders, make sure that the employees know that your reward system is fair.

> A UK food manufacturer surveyed employees and found that the majority felt demoralised because they were poorly paid. In reality,

the company paid higher salaries than 90 per cent of its competitors. I feel only communication was the key differentiator here. It transforms a good company and leader into a great one.

Firstly, fairness of rewards is an important issue for all employees. Secondly, if the organisation is not communicative in sending the right message to the team members, they start communicating among themselves, which in most cases is twisted and negative. Needless to say, this will break the morale, and the team will collapse. I again reiterate that communication is the most important factor between a good and a great company. It is time that we, as people leaders, learn to sell ourselves and our thoughts in an appropriate way.

Engage #1.1   Communicate, communicate, and again communicate.

Engage #2   Create a culture of collective management and celebrate each other's success.

I would love to mention Disney world here. I was fortunate to attend one of their trainings and realised that they had no monetary reward system. They had a concrete system of appreciating each other. Couldn't believe it.

Last month, while travelling through Europe, I was again fortunate to have a look at the real Disney world. It was true. How they appreciated each other in the cafeteria, patted on each other's backs, signed for each other, and supported and smiled for each other, was live.

It is their shear motivation through engagement to keep each visitor happy, engaged, and satisfied, with a 'wow' when he leaves the park, which creates the 'Disney Magic'. This is the 'magic' I am talking about throughout my book.

People leaders everywhere undervalue the power of spot recognition; in simple terms, appreciating team members on their efforts. This can be done by recognising any out-of-turn effort by just simply giving members gifts like dinner with his/her spouse or partner or with the chairman or a senior leader, tickets to a play or a sporting event, etc.

In the current scenario, if they complete a project on time and within budget, there should be a reward for it. The benefit is huge for the organisation. The cost is small in relation to it.

With these positive thoughts, we would look at what you have been waiting for so long; findings and recommendation for Gen Y.

The journey is going to get more exciting every minute hereon. We would next look at the new engagement model 'match the age' to 'keep them engaged', step by step. Let's stay focussed and enjoy the ride.

Key Learnings

Team members remain engaged, when given an opportunity to learn and grow, and are empowered to take critical decisions. Social security is equally important to them. One size does not fit all and that's the reason why 'matching the age' was born. Team goals are more important than individual goals in the overall scheme of things. An 'ideal worker' tag should not depend on age but on performance. 'Work and life balance' boosts performance and is one of the most important factor to 'keep them engaged', across generations.

People leaders should concentrate on how investment in employees will affect the bottom line of the organisation. We falter normally in Asian cultures, when we are asked to distinguish between a performer and a non-performer. Team members notice this quickly. Spot recognition is another important tool for boosting engagement.

CHAPTER 9

'Match the Age': Engaging Gen Y*

Key Objectives

- 'Matching the age' and defining it for Gen Y
- The Gen Y difference
- Gen Y: how to 'keep them engaged'?
- Are you repelling a Gen Y?
- General myths on Gen Y
- Influencers to 'keep them engaged'
- Value chain of 'keeping them engaged'
- Gen Y: 'engaged' v/s 'disengaged'
- Gen Y: 'keep them engaged' with the right drivers
- Certain examples from real-life situations and how they were dealt with?

> A new cluster of people can bring in a change, even if the movie is a remake. Similarly, there are people backstage who help in the final outcome of the movie.

Fresh ideas, virgin thoughts, and different outlooks, are always welcomed. To bring in drastic change in our overall outlook, we need to let these changes give impetus to our Gen Y so that we can move ahead and compete with the world.

I am again asking you: do you enjoy working with the young generation? Do you have it in you? If so, act. You will have plenty of opportunities, to contribute in the coming years. The generation, which is popularly known as Generation Y, and

---

*Gen Y: Employees below the age groups of 30 years

is below 30 years of age, will soon represent the biggest chunk of the Indian workforce. We are very fortunate to have these upcoming young and educated leaders, who will take India to where it was thousands of years ago.

We need to really stress on the need to make this workforce highly skilled and stress free. To produce great results and to make them highly productive, we need to understand their needs and engage them as their mentors. They are unique and are the greatest strength of our economy, and can be turned into a potent weapon for overall success.

Taking this into account, entrepreneurial leaders must ensure that the cynical Generation X, comprising of age groups 31 to 45 years, are managed well, as they are the grumpiest with the young ones. I have often noticed that they spend less time on connecting than correcting. Gen X finds their younger colleagues to be inconsistent, chipped, and sometimes incapable, with huge egos.

Entrepreneurial leaders should make quick changes to ensure productivity. We need to communicate with the other three generations openly, lay down our expectations in black and white, and explain their deliverables. People leaders would agree that the degree of challenge would vary according to the 'ideal worker's' strength and the overall core values of the organisation.

The previous generation leaders definitely have took a step towards it; let's together put the feet on the paddle. To do so, let's first look at some of the facts and then proceed further.

9.1 Let's look at some of the interesting traits of the Gen Y ('matching the age')

Entrepreneurial leaders should take note of the following traits, highlighting the difference of Gen Y from the other generations.

Match #1   Interestingly, about 65 per cent of Gen Y says that it is a priority for them to make the world a better place. Did we, belonging to the Gen X, ever think about it? My personal opinion would be a no. I was busy strengthening my own career.

Match #2   More than 70 per cent of the Gen Y would like to be their own bosses. Alarming! Can we look at the concepts of entrepreneurial employees? May be yes.

Match #3   Entrepreneurial leaders please note what they expect from you. More than 80 per cent of Gen Y would want their bosses to serve more as a coach or a mentor. They need a leader who is a subject matter expert, and also a friend.

Match #4   Shockingly, about 90 per cent of the Gen Y prefers a collaborative work culture, rather than a competitive one. Are you shocked? This is a fact and not a myth. With the advent of games and technology, we have mates in the virtual world with whom we share our valuable knowledge and time. This enhances the spirit of teamwork in the Gen Y.

Taking a clue from this, we should use games in form of learning exercises (also known as gamify in human resources), and build sessions around team building, which are completely innovative, exercise based, and outdoor. Armies across the globe use this practice, by creating situations closer to real life. Paint ball is a great example of one of the corporate games used for tactical team building.

Match #5   In my survey, more than 75 per cent of the Gen Y wanted flexible work schedules. I personally think that achievement v/s targets are more important than spending 12 hours on the desk. Other overhead expenses can also be reduced if flexible times can be initiated. But then again, it depends on the nature of business and the core value system of the organisation. It may not work in a manufacturing set-up or hospitals, as it may in an IT or consulting projects.

Match #6   About 90 per cent of the Gen Y wants 'work-life combination' too, which isn't the same as work-life balance. Work and life are now integrated, and are together indistinct.

Entrepreneurial leaders would have worked with 'venture capitalists'. Gen Y are in spirit, quite similar to them. They're not looking to fill any slot in an organisation. You will agree with me that every good businessman would invest in a start-up after looking at the difference, in terms of contribution to the society. Gen Y, look for similar things. Does it give you a hint on how to market, target your websites, career sections, etc.? This may seem like wishful thinking, particularly in the eyes of Gen X.

Entrepreneurial leaders can help Gen Y in a big way. They have to find ways to coach them to be better employees. The expectations have to be laid in such a way that it makes actual sense to them. I strongly recommend a path of coaching/mentoring, though they both are different. We should clearly lay down our expectations, thus, helping them to perform ideally.

Difference between coaching and mentoring

Coaching comes from the world of sports. Here, a coach coaches a team of players who definitely have some skills and knowledge. The players are in the team because of the same. His/her job is to ensure that the fine tuning of skills, and more so attitude, is worked on. The coach is not the one who would play Bret Lee or score goals. It is the team who needs to deliver on the field.

Mentoring is a little different, as in most cases, we try and change the character of a human being. We are trying to change something which develops till the age of seven, i.e., the character of a person. We try to convert whatever negative they have into positive energy.

It requires loads of work, it is time consuming, and requires a lot of effort. Dr. Kiran Bedi's work in Tihar is a prime example of mentoring and converting characters, from negative energy to positive. There are experts like counsellors or psychologists who correct relationships or your behaviour through continuous sessions of mentoring/counselling. It is not easy, as you need to unlearn, relearn, and learn.

To keep Gen Y engaged, you need to be a good teacher, explainer, coach and you should be able to answer them technically and logically. Remember your school days? Who was the best teacher you had? What were his/her qualities? If you list the top 2–3 qualities, you will definitely have the answer to the question. Listening skills, subject matter expertise, and the power to explain a difficult concept on the white board easily would distinctively be at the top of the list. Yes, these are the qualities which a manager needs to have when aligned with Gen Y. Their leader should be a mentor and a friend to them.

9.2 'Matching the age' and defining Gen Y

To make an impact in Gen Y's life, let us first understand the critical differences and characteristics of this unique generation.

46 years plus or baby boomers, are currently one of the largest generation of active workers in India. If we list down their strengths, it would be longevity, positivity, and their enthusiasm to put in long hours. Gen Y is poles apart; they are well-educated, skilled in tools, very confident, are able to multi-task, and bundled with loads of positive energy.

They have high expectations for themselves, and are always ready to work in teams, rather than as individuals. Leaders should make a note that, though work and life balance is of utmost importance for them, they are ready for challenges. Their need for social interaction and immediate results differentiate them from Gen X, who are closest to their heels, in terms of technology.

In India, we need to look at 'matching the age' more seriously, as the Gen Y is the largest age group to emerge significantly. They would comprise of the largest proportion of the workforce in the next 8–10 years. It is also important to note that teenagers in schools and colleges will by then, be the working class of Gen Y. As leaders, we need to be a step ahead in preparation. I call them as 'one-click generation'.

Leaders will need to make major adjustments in their engagement models. Leaders will have to carefully consider what strategies they will use to engage and retain valuable workforce of the Gen Y now, and into the future?

I also feel that with the advent of technology and keeping in mind the overall nature of Gen Y, some exciting engagement, and out-of-the-box solutions would be invented, as we move ahead.

9.3 What's is so different in Gen Y ('match the age')?

Entrepreneurial leaders would have noticed that millennial are creating a change in how work gets done, as they work more in teams and use more technology. Almost 70 per cent say that giving back and being civically involved are their utmost priorities. Gen Y is very creative and has information at the back of their hands. They are also very inquisitive in nature, and their hunger to know more and experiment with the knowledge, makes them more creative.

Today, my 15 year old son can talk to my friends in the US, who design aircraft engines, talk to me about football clubs, discusses the Renaissance period and Socrates, can speak in French, and get us back to the hotel when we were lost in Paris; speak about Formula 1 cars, etc.

Rishi's IQ, I must admit, is far higher than mine, at the same age. How is it possible? It is because of the availability of knowledge with a click of a button, and the ability to be inquisitive, which makes a difference.

Through a Google or Wiki search, answers to complicated questions can be found. Gen Y wants to work on new and tough problems, and ones that require creative solutions. They have clarity in their thoughts and expectations. They will say no directly, which is what I love in them.

We, as their teachers or parents, have also inculcated the habit of asking questions and gaining more information. So, as a leader, I should be prepared to have an answer to all the bouncers coming my way.

In my previous roles, I have seen leaders making a mistake here. They always assumed and faltered. On the excuse of experience, leaders gave Gen Y a rough deal, less meaningful jobs, and thus, disengaging them thoroughly. Along with appreciation, every leader should be able to face the toughest questions too.

Many a time, I have seen a senior employee mistrusting a Gen Y, suspecting that he/she lacks commitment. My question here is, how can we judge them so accurately, if we do not even give them proper work opportunities or roles to perform?

The younger generation employee is interested in timely feedback on his or her performance. Traditional, semi-annual or annual reviews are too infrequent for Gen Y. They want the next role in six months to a year. They want to know that whether or not they have done a good job. I strongly second their thoughts. A timely evaluation is far better than waiting for the mid-term appraisals or year-end ones, so that they can correct themselves.

I suggest that a leader should just reach out to them and their resolution, so that their prospective is taken into account. It is important to then convey your ideas with reasoning, and I am sure 99 per cent of the times, you will become good in their books.

This list is endless. A perfect leader should offer plenty of help; reward them on regular basis for being innovative; encourage them to take risks and if they are lost, and show them the right path. Engage them with frequent and timely feedback, be mentors to them, create a shared and team-favour slanted culture, and you would see the difference. Feedback must also be given in such a way that millennial are receptive to it.

> In one of my previous roles, I started a process of monthly job chats, to ensure that we were in line with them. With management trainees, I started personal weekly chats.
>
> Though a little out of context, but I firmly believe in the alignment of the chairman's vision with his leadership team through a weekly or fortnightly exercise. Non alignment in both cases can be very costly.

This generation is well-connected through just the word-of-mouth or social networking. It is much easier to spread good or bad news out of the office premises, with the click of a button. Every transaction with them is a moment of truth.

> A sandwich benefit statement is used by salesmen across the globe. Like a sandwich, which has two breads and a filling, salesmen use this technique to make features into benefits for the customers. Similarly, they insert a feature, like a filling between two benefits, like bread.
>
> The good feedback technique is very similar to the sandwich benefit statement. Leaders need to use two positive feet forward, and insert one area of improvement, like a sandwich. Leaders just need to be precise and to the point, when giving such feedback.
>
> At Viraj, one of my achievements was post-appraisal feedback, to each and every employee. It is important post appraisal to let each employee know where he/she is lagging behind or doing good, and how can he/she improve.

9.4 How to 'keep them engaged' (Gen Y) especially in this competitive and tough scenario?

In this chapter, I have shared a lot of personal experience, arising out of dealing with Gen Y. You are requested to look at it from your organisational point of view, and then implement them. Always believe in your ideas, however small they may appear.

I have tried to identify which engagement drivers were fitting for each generation. Using both, quantitative analyses, which utilised employee engagement survey data from respondents in five companies, as well as qualitative interviews, I compiled conclusions that are relevant for senior leaders, responsible for engagement policies.

The full list of drivers and threats measured in the study were, value system of the organisation, superiority in relation to competition, opportunities to learn and grow through career progression, aiding environment which continually supports performance, work and life balance, and measurable and attainable booty month on month.

The leaders in the survey feedback felt that macro scale management and clarity, and more responsibility to line managers, would help. I think each one of us would support what my learned colleagues have echoed. They also felt that team members with 30 odd years of exposure will have to readapt be more flexible, and work in teams.

The study of Gen Y is interesting, as their needs are different from the perception of the other generations.

9.5 The first important question that we need to answer: are we repelling Gen Y?

Do any of your leaders express the following view of Gen Y?

View #1   Gen Y have a false sense of power and over exaggerated sense of their knowledge and skills.

View #2 Gen Y have a whimsically high outlook for their own career progression. They feel they want to be in the senior management in five years. They feel it is too less a time to grow into a senior role.

View #3 Gen Y have no organisational dependability. They are here as trespassers.

View #4 Gen Y are lethargic, lacking principles, ethics, and emotional intelligence. It is surprising that the IQ scores are improving year on year. I don't think only academics are responsible for it. It might also be Internet; leading to the one-click generation.

View #5 Gen Y hate hard work or compensating their salaries paid to them in literal words.

Take these leaders through numbers, facts, and graphs of engagement surveys and trends across the globe, or even in the Indian scenario. For organisational progress, it is important for leadership teams to identify these leaders, build faith in them, and then take them through some of the heart-burning facts and figures. Try and change their thought process and perspective towards Gen Y. A mentoring technique may help.

It would be time consuming, but in the long run, the alignment of these generations will be worth millions of dollars. These leaders are required to pass on the skills and problem-solving capabilities to these young members of the Gen Y.

9.6 Let's now look at the general myths on Gen Y and find out if they really exist in reality

Is it necessary to have a senior or a proven actor to make a blockbuster? If it was so, we would have never had debuts, and you would have not been reading this book.

Let's now look at the top three general myths around Gen Y:

- Myth #1 They lack organisational faithfulness: In my findings, the result was different. I found them equally loyal to any other age group, if not more.

- Myth #2 They are only motivated by perks and money: In my research, I found that motivation is based more on personality, than on age. They were motivated to join and contribute in organisations which contributed to the society. If that's the thought process, we all know that these organisations are stable; roles can be interesting, but these organisations are not high pay masters. It was also shocking that Gen X themselves highly rated this as a motivator. Circumstances and situations also contribute to the overall ratings.

- Myth #3 Gen Y has no respect for specialists: Different people have different definitions of respect, which may cause disharmony. They were found willing to learn if treated and mentored in a right way.

9.7 Influencers for Gen Y to 'keep them engaged'

As leaders, we must know what this generation stands for. We should identify their influencers, and then plan engagement interventions around it. Please remember they are 'the future'.

Through studies and research, I could identify nine major influencers, and our 'keeping them engaged' plan at an organisational level should consider these important indicators:

Indicator #1   They are going to be the largest workforce in India.

Indicator #2   Highly training driven.

Indicator #3   Most educated female demographics in the history of the country.

Indicator #4   Most tech savvy even in their daily lives.

Indicator #5   They are bold and courageous to face all challenges.

Indicator #6   On-the-job learners.

Indicator #7   Love to work in teams.

Indicator #8   Trained by the society to contribute ideas: Open to stop you and share with you what they think is right. I personally love this characteristic the most. It is a real challenge and fun to facilitate them.

Indicator #9   In the real world, not so emotional in the overall approach to life. Senior generations should learn this from Gen Y.

130

9.8 Value Chain: 'keeping them engaged'

In Figure 9.1, we look from an entrepreneurial angle the value chain of Gen Y. It leads to a direct impact on balance sheet.

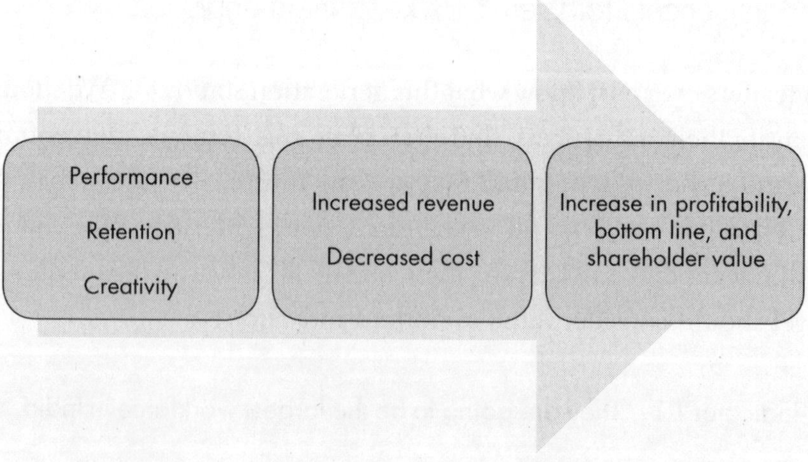

Performance

Retention

Creativity

Increased revenue

Decreased cost

Increase in profitability, bottom line, and shareholder value

FIGURE 9.1   Value chain: 'keeping them engaged'

9.9 Engaged v/s disengaged Gen Y (benefits to 'keep them engaged')

Engage #1 More than 30 per cent of engaged Gen Y are more likely to achieve their tasks.

Engage #2 More than 65 per cent of engaged Gen Y are more likely to contribute to the organisation's goals.

Engage #3 About 100 per cent of younger workers are more likely to put extra effort or hours.

In Figure 9.2, we can clearly see the needs of this young generation, and these top enablers easily improve their efficiency by their age-specific needs. As leaders, we need to build our solutions, and nurture this generation around these numbers.

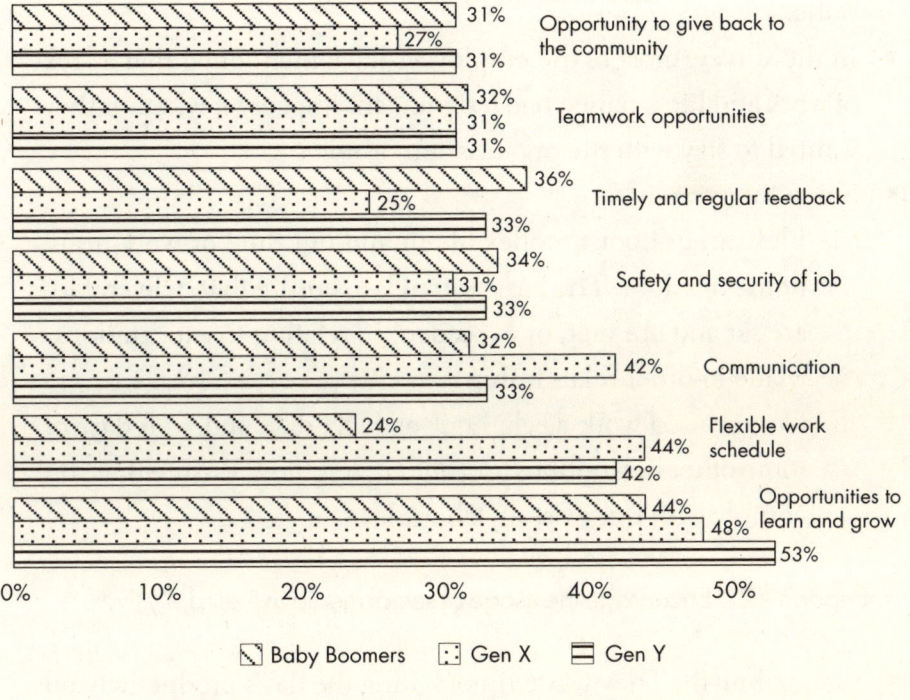

FIGURE 9.2 Benefits to 'keep them engaged'

9.10 Solutions: Gen Y – 'keeping them engaged' with the right drivers, and creating 'the magic'

> The entire production unit is looking after the comfort of its actors. If the actors are not happy and engaged, the performance quality would be affected. On similar lines, we need to treat our employees as stars. Engaging these stars would have a positive impact on the final product or service.

It is far better to invest in our employees and devise methods to retain them innovatively. As leaders, let us focus on creating 'the magic' through thirteen different channels by 'keeping them engaged'.

Engage #1 Sensitivity to work pressures, especially in 24X7 environments, by providing flexible work options.

- More than 80 per cent of Gen Y wants to be mobile, rather than static.
- In the survey, most of the employees have mentioned that a lack of work and life balance had a significant impact on whether they wanted to stay with the organisation or not.
- Some Suggestions:
    i. Flexi-time: Look at a flexible in and out time or work-from-home freedom. The basic intent is to ensure that deliverables are set and are met, or exceeded, in relation to expectations.
    ii. Made-to-order relationship
    iii. Compressed work week: Look at 12X4 days and 3 off days or some other best options for your organisation. Ensure that you comply with our existing labour laws.

Engage #2 Encourage the usage of social media in their daily lives.

- General myth: They waste time, killing the day's productivity on social media.

- My studies showed that employees, who served less than 10 per cent of time on net, were less productive than employees who served 20 per cent time on the internet.
- Some suggestions:
  i. Train on core business technologies: This group believes in sticking to an organisation, which gives them more learning opportunities. Individual career paths should be focussed on individual development needs. Make them different from the market by treating them as a bucket of talent. Create a niche in them and upgrade their skills. They will stick to your organisation.
  ii. Encourage them to use social media as a learning tool.
  iii. If you as a leader restrict internet, they will use their smart phones. No need to overly restrict it. The policies like no internet, no chats, etc., do not work anymore. Rather than they hiding from you and doing the same, it is better to open it up for them. Definitely you should block a few unwanted sites, but never block social sites, ticketing, and shopping sites.

    Monitor how much time each computer spends on the net, and how much on real-time work. If counselling is required, go ahead. Behave like a friend and a parent. If you can't give them internet access in the workspace, give it to them separately in a room or cafeteria. Let them use it in free time. Monitor break timings and the number of breaks. Productivity will improve with empowerment. I have seen this many times.

    Leveraging technology effectively for business use is different than using it for personal use. Educate them.

Engage #3   Creating and enabling environment with on-the-job preparations, by virtue of continuous upgradation of skills, and by finding alternate ways.

- General myth: They are only interested in money.
    i. As per the survey results, Gen Y has chosen development three times over salary. Interestingly, the same was ranked as the number one skill desired from a leader.
- Some suggestions:
    i. Constant development: learning and development plays a critical role in their retention. They love to upgrade their skills. Just ensure as leaders that they contribute out of their learnings. If they upgrade, they should become mentors, buddies, or trainers, for the new set of Gen Y. Give them responsibility and trust them.
    ii. Mentoring and coaching: mentoring can be used for new hires with buddy programmes or attachment with an SME.

> While doing a green belt project in IBM, I realised that we could reduce the induction training by a few days. The new batches had time, and also, nine hours of continuous training daily, is like torture.
>
> We mixed six hours of theory, with two hours of daily listening to calls in a call centre. Listening to these calls and how were they handled gave them practical knowledge. Also, it killed the boring schedule.
>
> The next batch onwards, we could reduce the overall time by two days, and also improve on the pass percentage of batches, and their quality scores.

    iii. Stretch assignments: they want to be given more responsibilities; just give it to them. Monitor depending on their maturity levels.
    iv. Training others: Some of them handle people, media, and technology, very well. Get them to do what they love doing.
    v. Job shadows: Aligning youngsters with a subject matter expert, in their field of interest, would help their overall growth. The mentor should be an 'ideal teacher', accommodating their

views, thus grooming them and enabling them to become better professionals and productive workers.

Engage #4   Evidence of career progression and skills upgradation, by mapping their individual career paths, developmental needs, etc., into a common bundle.

- General myth: The common belief is that, Gen Y has no loyalty. It is both untrue and unfair.
- In my survey, leaders and sometimes even the organisations are not loyal to employees.
- Team members are unsure and are good at the early stage of their careers. This statement is so true. In the beginning of our careers, we were also not sure of the same. Isn't it wrong to blame them?
- The employees of all age groups are moving around. Interestingly, one out of every three employees in India is looking for a change. World average would soon hit 12–15 jobs in a career span. Why blame them? If you and your organisation are good, you would be able to retain them.
- Some suggestions:
  i. Create and communicate individual career paths and trainee career paths. You can also create fast-track career paths for A-listed college pass outs.
  ii. Do not go back on what you promise in the campus. Do your homework as a leader, be in agreement, and then hit the campus.
  iii. It is important to engage them post their offer letters. We had discussed one such example in the previous chapter. Read it again and you will know what I am trying to say. It gives you a clear cut action plan on how to engage between offers and joining.
  iv. Map it out in consultation with them. Their developmental plan should be a two-way communication.

Let me take you through a very interesting learning. In one of the organisations, we had both, management training and operational training programmes. Operational training programme was a level below the management training programme. Students from similar backgrounds were picked for both the programmes. What was the key differentiator between two students, selected for different programmes, but from the same college? It was sometimes noticed that a management training programme entrant was just exceptional on the day of interview.

Some of my operational trainees were exceptional at work. I was forced to convince the leadership team to review the one year training period, and then re-evaluate new incumbents on consistent performance. We upgraded many operational trainees after a year of constant performance. It was a very positive way of keeping all the trainees performing, and on their feet for one year.

v. Create communities of common interests.

vi. Gamify the interventions and developmental activities.

vii. As entrepreneurial leaders, innovate at every stage.

> For example, when you hired a graduate engineering batch from an A-grade college, they needed to be knit into a team. We should then plan for them extraordinary activity-driven off site induction or a theatre, which breaks the fear of failure.

Engage #5   Fairness of booty, measurable benefits, and their timely distribution through rewards and recognition. Working on individual compensations or flexible options (keep the option open for them to decide).

- Gen Y is motivated by service awards. Interestingly though, they think of performance and not tenure. We all thought service awards are medals for long-term services; for them it means performance.

- They want to be recognised in a way that they value.
- Some suggestions:
    i. Recognition should be preferred over rewards. We have spoken about the example of Disney, and how the team members motivate and celebrate each other's success.
    ii. Even if other generations say so, Gen Y was not motivated with booty or cash rewards.
    iii. If you ask me, I have never seen one person in the last two decades, who has been satisfied with his/her current remuneration. Then why do people stick with reputed brands like Tata, even when they pay lower than the competition?
    iv. Include developmental opportunities into rewards.
    v. Customised or personalised rewards are the best. Try and work towards one-to-one reward mechanism. An example can be in the form similar to a personal credit card.
    vi. Timely distribution of the reward also is very important, especially in the current circumstances.

The best would be a point system like a credit card, where they can accumulate points. Make the point table more interesting, by probably adding 25 points for every work anniversary, rather than the date of birth. The team members should be in a position to claim these rewards when they need to.

Engage #6   Ethics and conduct of leaders, and open door policy, works the best for Gen Y

- Gen Y should always be encouraged to be part of the conversations, as they like to share ideas. You may like to reward the brilliant ideas they generate in some form or the other.
- They want to shadow their senior managers and learn from them.
- Some suggestions:

i. Meet and greet: let them meet leaders on achievements (leaders like the MD or the chairman whom they don't see often).

ii. Namaskar meeting: We started with this new concept. On day one of common joining, we have an evening cup of coffee with the leadership team. Even a few lunches together with leaders, made a lot of difference. Leaders have positive vibes and vision. Gen Y loves informal, yet effective ways of communication.

iii. Case competitions.

iv. Town halls.

v. Social media or similar interest group get-togethers.

vi. Mentoring tips.

Engage #7   Feeling to be part of the success story. Be a brand leader through innovation and contribution.

- More than 50 per cent of the Gen Y confirmed that they will start their own business if they lose or get into any trouble in job.
- Interestingly, this is up from the world data of approximately 30 per cent in 2009.
- Can we use this to our benefit? Yes, this is a very good sign, as we can implant the seeds of entrepreneurial leadership skills in Gen Y.
- Some suggestions:
    i. Firstly, build a culture of entrepreneurial employees.
    ii. Create team rooms.
    iii. Line the walls with thought-provoking material.
    iv. Think out of the box and let them innovate.

Conduct a painting competition, with the best paintings to be framed in conference rooms.

We created a similar competition for the children of employees; selected 12 best ones, made an executive dairy out of it, and distributed it as a New Year gift across the industry and clients.

The engagement with families across was evident.

v. Allow a certain amount of time for employee-driven work.

vi. Encourage leaders to host brainstorming sessions.

Engage #8 Core values of the organisation and its leadership team should be able to connect them to the big picture or ecosystems at an organisation level.

- Gen Y grew up with an education system changing in India and with encouraged critical thinking. Learning methods have changed over years, though the training methods are constant.
- Parents encourage questions in them. Leaders should treat them as their own children. Empathise with them.
- Gen Y needs the task to employ and put forth l their logic, or they will disengage.
- Some suggestions:
  i. Have a leader who can communicate what is being done at an organisational level and why.
  ii. Answer their questions timely.
  iii. Communicate possible changes before they happen.
  iv. Communicate to them how they would contribute to better the world.
  v. Listen to their feedback.
  vi. Incorporate their good suggestions.

Engage #9 Celebrate each other's success and facilitate a community atmosphere.

- More than 90 per cent of Gen Y said that they wanted co-workers who are fun to work with.
- Approximately 80 per cent felt that they enjoy in common activity-driven communities.
- Other generations did not put the above mentioned two points in their list of top five desires.

- Gen Y employees ranked the same above luxurious office spaces, state-of-art technology, and even surprisingly, work and life balance.
- Some suggestions:
  i. Wherever possible, recruit likeminded people, and people who can smile.
  ii. Sponsor team-building events and trainings. Sponsor similar interest groups. Create forums of choice or hobbies, and let them be a part of it.
  iii. Divide them into houses like in school, and have a competition for the cup running.
  iv. Make sports clubs, select teams, and participate with them in corporate tournaments. Get one of your suppliers to sponsor you in the tournament, if you do not have the budget for it.
  v. Ask employees who would like responsibilities, and give it to them. Give them budgetary restrictions with it.
  vi. Leaders should participate in interconnecting events with them.

Engage #10   Promote a genuine best employer brand, or aim to be one of the best places to work

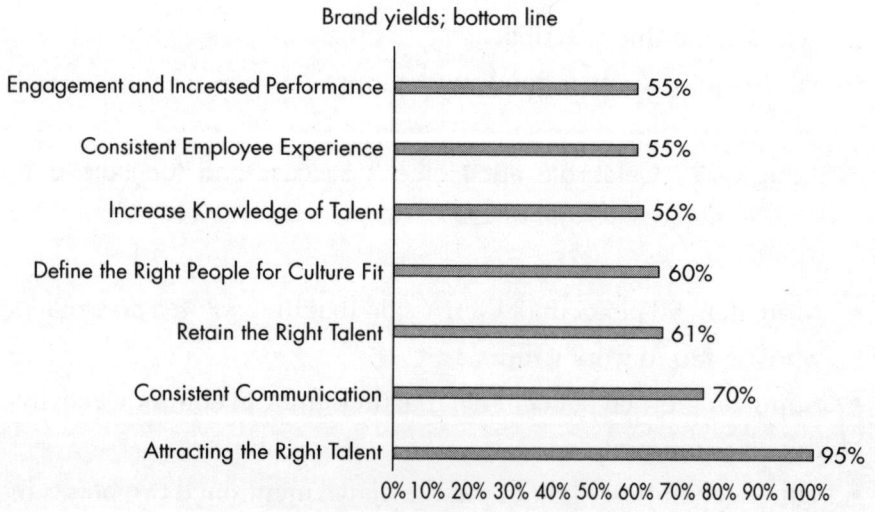

Brand yields; bottom line

Engagement and Increased Performance	55%
Consistent Employee Experience	55%
Increase Knowledge of Talent	56%
Define the Right People for Culture Fit	60%
Retain the Right Talent	61%
Consistent Communication	70%
Attracting the Right Talent	95%

0% 10% 20% 30% 40% 50% 60% 70% 80% 90% 100%

FIGURE 9.3   Brand yields

- Some suggestions:
    i. A strong employer brand will make your organisation distinct from the other competitive employers.
    ii. They will disengage if the organisation is not living up to its promise. Always under-promise and over-deliver.
    iii. They may use social media to broadcast their thoughts.
    iv. It is important if you go for one of these surveys after working towards it. Getting a top rank in the best places to work list will reflect your commitment and intent.

Engage #11   Professional evaluation of the progress through timely and prompt feet forward.

- Leaders must switch their perspective of management from being job critics and assessors to teachers in the current scenario.
- More than 80 per cent of Gen Y wanted regular feet forward and recognition. Timely feet forward is the key to their engagement.
- Everyone in this generation believes that for their development, they should be attached to strong coaches and mentors.
- Some suggestions:
    i. Timely feet forward is important.
    ii. Schedule quarterly evaluations; if possible, monthly job chats with no impact on appraisals. That would be the best.
    iii. Involve them in skip-level meetings, conduct open houses, share a feedback online, online help desks, etc.
    iv. Let them build their own training needs by getting a 360 degrees appraisal.
    v. Insist that the managers attached to them are open to lots of questions and feedback.
    vi. Walk the talk, have an open door policy, and prove it to them.
    vii. Ideate and give them some time to ideate for the organisation, irrespective of the nature of their jobs or departments. Do not lay boundaries while ideating. Companies like Google do it very well.

Engage #12   Mentorship: it is the key for Gen Y

- As per my studies, more than 80 per cent of Gen Y wanted their leaders to be mentors or coaches.
- Some suggestions:
    i. Identify the skills they are good at. Involve them in mentoring others in the skills they are good at. For example, social media, technology shortcuts, process reviews, etc.
    ii. They can bring new enabling ideas to the table.
    iii. They can mentor the recruitment process for other members of Gen Y.
    iv. If they are happy, they can be the change agents. They can also get you loads of referrals, as they are very well connected.

Engage #13   Make them socially accountable and thereby, build the overall organisational culture.

- Gen Y doesn't necessarily need you to be saving the planet, but they would like to know whether the organisation is up to with times.
- As per my studies, about 50 per cent liked water-saving devices.
- Survey showed that 70 per cent liked to share printers in the office.
- More than 70 per cent liked to have recycling bins.
- More than 50 per cent would like stand-by devices on all electrical equipment.
- These are Indian numbers, and not very far (+-2per cent) from global numbers.
- Some suggestions:
    i. Ask your employees for their inputs. Every penny saved is every penny earned. Reward them innovatively. For example, you can reward them with 5 per cent of the savings from their suggested projects.

ii. Give your employees one paid volunteer day per year.
 iii. Create an employee customer engagement programme.
 iv. Provide employees an opportunity to work with the CSR team.
  v. Involve the leadership team in CSR activities.

Real-life examples

I have shared many examples during the chapter. But, at the end of it, I would like to share some interesting, real-life situations, and how I handled them as a leader. Please look at these closely, check for fitment with your organisational culture, and then implement them in your workplace.

Challenge #1   Expectations at work, and the availability of tools to continuously produce quality output – Example from the ITES and the hospitality industry

Solution: We started monthly job chats. It was an informal way of raising the concern and identifying those concerns. As a leader, your main motto should be to close loop these concerns.

I took it to the next level by communicating the same, and also by communicating the employees the reasons for not closing certain tickets.

Communication is the key differentiator.

Challenge #2   Work and life balance – Example from the ITES and the hospitality industry

Taking a clue from concierges for guests, we started an employee concierge. It had such a positive impact, and in the real sense, employees were benefited

After real long hours of work, they did not had to bother about bill payments, groceries, forms, banking, ticketing, etc. It was a great success from day 1.

Challenge #3   Vision alignment of leaders with the chairman and the MD

143

We realised that there is a gap between the vision of our chairman and the leadership team. So we started a fortnightly chat for the leadership team and quarterly appraisal. I always believe that the chairman's direct reportees should always be aligned with him/her. They are his/her veins and need to circulate the same to all the teams.

Challenge #4   Vision alignment – A very big hospitality organisation
Is it difficult to remember 10–12 words vision statements and align with them?

When we are not a part of the process, we do not remember the same. I started with a simple exercise, by asking the leadership team members to draw the vision on a chart paper with colours without using a word, logo, or alphabets. They had to explain what they had drawn on the chart.

Once you draw it, you would always be aligned to it. We implemented the same at an organisation level, started the same exercise in all regions, workshops, forums, inductions, town halls, Skype, etc.

In the next step, I made all the stakeholders sign on the vision statement and framed it. When you can see your signature in the conference hall, you will always be aligned with it.

With these examples, I hope I have implanted some seeds of fresh thoughts in your ecosystems. I would like to bring to your notice that these are very specific cases, and would request you that before implementing any such specific engagement intervention or solutions, take a look at your organisation's values, culture, and your target 'ideal employees'. Look for their fitment into the overall scheme of things.

In the subsequent chapter, we would look at the interesting characteristics of the next generation, Gen X, and how to engage them.

Key Learnings

We can compete with the world, as we are going to have one of the youngest workforce. The responsibility is on us to provide them with the correct learning opportunities, pass on the baton, and groom them for the future. Interestingly, the younger lot wants to contribute to make the world a better place. They also wish to be their own bosses, work in teams, have flexible work-life options, and dedicatedly invest in their careers.

Their mentors need to have all characteristics of an exceptionally good school teacher. The most important factor for them is timely feedback. I have seen that they are so well connected socially, and any form of positive or negative word can spread like wild fire. I say without any doubt that the younger generation is simply splendid. Interestingly, 'keeping them engaged' is so beneficial for the organisation because, most of the engaged youngsters put in extra efforts in their jobs.

CHAPTER 10

'Match the Age': Engaging Gen X*

Key Objectives

- 'Match the age': defining Gen X.
- 'Match the age' — Gen X: differences and challenges.
- Basic characters of Gen X and their differentiators.
- Gen X: how to motivate and 'keep them engaged'.
- 'Matching the age' and training the Gen X.

10.1 'Match the age': differences and challenges (Gen X)

Taking it forward from where we left, managing multi-generational or diverse workforces is an art.

> Handling a multi-starrer movie, with stars having different needs, is difficult.
> Young workers want to make a quick impact, the middle generation needs to believe in the mission, and the older employees don't like inconsistency.

'Matching the age' and understanding differences in diverse workplaces is critically important, as each generation has

---

*Gen X: Employees between the age group of 31 to 45 years

difference experiences which induces specific likings, beliefs, principles, and styles of work. We Gen X are different from baby boomers.

Another major difference in this age, or the need of the hour is what I call a sense of self-pride, ego, or the need for recognition. This generates different behavioural patterns and styles of working in Gen X.

I am a firm advocate of the performance being driven mostly by this group. They are your organisation's drivers, first line supervisors, or line managers. Gen X is also your hands and eyes on the shop floor in modern times. Their mood swings or signs of dissatisfaction may not be good news for entrepreneurial leaders. This group needs to be happy, engaged, trained, and delivering consistently.

Last but not the least, the challenging issue they bring to the table is in terms of their overall behaviour towards younger generation and elder ones. Being very critical, they give the least scores on engagement matrices to other generations. On the other hand, they are very quick to recognise the initiatives and contribution of their own generation towards the objectives of the organisation.

10.2 Basic characteristics of Gen X by 'matching the age'

Match #1   Generation X is the first generation to grow up with blended families. Especially in Asian countries and cultures like India, where the majority of us are brought with a value system of respect. Gen X predominantly lived in joint families, but believed in value systems, which is also one of the reasons behind their dual nature.

For example if you look at us, we still believe and listen to our family leaders. In some Asian countries like Japan, it is stronger than even India. This can be used by leaders positively in case of engagement. Here, family needs and engagement should also be looked at in depth.

Match #2   This generation believed in freedom, elasticity, adaptability, and flexibility, more strongly than previous generations.

Match #3   Advent of technology started with this generation, and we have seen it develop gradually, from luxury to necessity. Example, instant messaging, blogs, internet, and multi-player games have generated new skills and styles of collaborating in Generations X and Y, to such a degree that it has made them different. Gen X, with their learning abilities, has been able to cope with the changes in technology.

Match #4   Gen X is challenged by the rigidity of the nine to six workdays.

Entrepreneurial leaders should note that Gen X has similar needs like Gen Y. Their engagement scores proved the same, though most of them pointed out family needs as priority. Thus, it is important for the organisations to plan engagement which suits family needs, apart from the employee. Let the families be engaged in the organisational functions like family picnics, informal get-togethers, etc. Getting them to know each other will increase the bonding and loyalty toward the company. Gifting children and their better halves will enhance the possibility of reducing attrition.

In my experience and limited knowledge, I have tried to build engagement interventions around their family needs.

While watching an award function on national network, something clicked which acted as magic, while implementing it. Let me tell you something about it.

The star attraction for our annual day function was our yearly awards. To surprise the winners, I secretly collected some video and sound bites, from their loved ones.

> We played them on the big screen as soon as the team members went to pick up the award.
>
> I remember seeing tears and emotions, and I received maximum hugs on that day. It was a dream comes true for me, as a leader.

That's why I always say that it is important to plan your engagement needs with open eyes and ears, and as per the requirement of your organisation, team, and the age of employees. Empathise with your team members and keep the positive energy flowing. Another important thing is to 'keep it changing', and ensure they are always kept guessing. Don't be monotonous; make it interesting.

Leaders, when we 'match the age', Gen X leads the pack when it comes to positive perception of both the characteristics and management skills. Members of Gen X were cited as the best among the generations in seven out of eleven attributes, including being profit creators, as well as owning traits of flexibility, difficult problem-solving abilities, and team partnership.

However, members from this age bracket lagged behind the elder generation in being perceived as the best at displaying managerial existence and cost effectiveness, which is quite obvious with experience and exposure.

While evaluating Gen X leaders, seven out of ten respondents said that they are best equipped to manage teams overall, compared to boomers at 25 per cent and Gen Y at 5 per cent.

10.3 Differentiators

From the survey, it was evident that through 'matching the age', Gen X follows the top eleven differentiators (not in any particular order).

Match #1   Techno-mastery: they are closest to Gen Y in techno-mastery.

Match #2   Self-containment: this group is self-contented and can perform without any support or interventions.

Match #3   Multi-tasking abilities: this is highest among all generations, though I always believed that women generally are more multi-skilled. They can speak to friends, cook, and watch TV simultaneously.

Match #4   Objective co-ordination: it is very easy for Gen X to bring into line, influence, and adjust them as per organisational requirement.

Match #5   Confident and optimistic approach.

Match #6   Impatience: this has to be tackled. Normally at this age, they have many issues at the back of their hands, like money, house, car, children's education, etc. For example a flexi policy of car to save their taxes would work best with this group.

Match #7   Need for flexible hours and informal work environment demands.

Match #8   Worldwide thinking and credit: a pat on the back and timely feedback are must.

Match #9   Easy stability, poise, and steadiness.

Match #10   Can-do attitude, but with independence: empower them, trust them, and communicate. You may see outstanding results in most cases.

Match #11   Capability to question the power: Let them be innovative and think out of the box. It is a good sign for the organisation. Just tell them to get two solutions for every problem, and it would be beneficial for you as a leader.

Other characteristics they reflected through various studies were as follows. They are interesting, and they will get you closer to these groups as an entrepreneurial leader:-

Match #1   They preferred casual business (low-end).

Match #2   Like flexible schedules.

Match #3   Carrot: job security and not salary.

Match #4   Mentoring: not interested to receive feedback.
They appreciated the quality of work of their subordinates and peers, but shockingly, were critical of superior's deliverables. This is an interesting and shocking news for most of the leaders. It also tells us that these supervisors also need behavioural and man-management lessons.

Match #5   Social security, measurable, and attainable booty month on month.

Match #6   Client and interaction: emails or chats or high-end phones. Their ego needs are very close to their hearts.

Match #7   Tools: creates own documents, uses mobiles and laptops, uses web to research, review, etc., e-mail or mobile 24X7.
It was astonishing to know that the amount of time they spend with their loved ones was less, and their need to be glued to something or the other was more. Approximately sleep hours were reduced from 7–8 hours to 6 hours in the last decade or so.

Does it affect the work? The answer is highly debatable, and we will keep it parked for now.

Match #8   Livelihood aims: build a variety of skills and experiences.

Match #9   They tend to avoid policies.
Business over other things is always there in their bloods.
We need to mentor them accordingly.

Faith in leadership needs to be installed in them, so that their people management skills are developed. They are like a double-edged sword, and how to tame them is the challenge of the hour.

Now, as a leader, you have seen the top indicators of Gen X and their overall behaviour. I hope that this data, in simple form, would make your life easier. Let's look at solutions that would help you as an entrepreneurial leader throughout your life. Let's try and look at the solution to create 'the magic'.

10.5 Gen X: how to motivate and 'keep them engaged'? (How to create 'the magic')

From my survey, it was evident that Gen X could be motivated by the following interventions:

Engage #1   Measurable and attainable booty month on month.
Entrepreneurial leaders would have realised by now that Gen X are generally not interested in traditional perks, and the same need to be individually aligned. Tax saving methods for instance, may give you a competitive edge.
The flexi options work best for this group. If we can make individual training needs, career paths, then why not individual engagement and perks. I want each one of you to

think on these lines. Leave a part of the booty open for them to decide, once in the beginning of the year, and once in middle. Won't it create 'the magic'? I think so.

Why I say so? From my experience, this age group is burdened with house loans, family, children, and sometimes ailing parents. Empower them to plan for themselves. Keep it just tax friendly, if possible, by law.

Engage #2   Distinguish a performer from a non-performer.

My suggestion is to have an individual career path in organisations, and definitely formulate distinguishing parameters between a key performer and a non-performer, in a mid or large organisation.

'The magic' would be created if there is a separate booty for difficult enactment, going out of the way.

I would like to give you a live example of in one of the organisations, I have worked for. We had a booty for difficult enactment. Apart from the CTC, which includes performance rewards in most cases and other perks, we had a chairman's booty or fund which is given to each group company based on the request of the respective MD for the same, and the performance of the arm.

The booty was known as as Performance Related Pay (PRP). This is awarded to employees doing a difficult job, out of their own cushion. Normally, these jobs are not part of their regular designated key result areas. Isn't it a very fantastic motivation tool? These rewards become more impactful if the recognition, and distribution is timely and unbiased.

Hotels sometimes require an exceptional talent like tandoor personnel to be retained. However, you cannot include them in the high potential employee category. A deferred bonus may work, in their case.

Again, it is different for different organisations. I feel that money is not the motivator, but sometimes, in some positions, it can work well.

Talking about pros and cons of the same, we should also look at the popular model and pay for performance categorically. The biggest corporation to come out of it in the recent times is Microsoft. But, in the Indian scenario, and especially in certain parts of the country, it is must-have to ensure continuous productivity.

Engage #3   'The magic' can be created by empowering Gen X, apart from giving them independence, and the same can be demolished by the lack of it.

Engage #4   'The magic' can also be created by gifting them a trendy phone, and I pad or a laptop, instead of money.

Engage #5   Gen X wants its leadership team to make it clear what their expectations are as a leader or an organisation. The set key result area should be mapped timely with their performance. Communicate to them as a leader and anticipate and allow them to perform. See the results with empowerment. People leaders should also note that lack of empowerment can be destructive. I strongly advocate hiring of talent and empowering them, because without empowerment, talent is ZERO.

Engage #6   Allowing them to question the experts and authorities can create confidence and conviction. Open door policy may create 'the magic'.

10.6 'Match the age' and train Gen X

However strong the actor is in his skills, he needs to read the script, get deep into the groove of the character, and has to be mentored by the director. A director moulds an actor to get desirable results.

An interesting part of this chapter deals with the training and coaching needs of Gen X. Some of you would question my intent.

The findings across the globe reflect the disengagement between Generations X and Y. We, as leaders, need to bridge it. We also have a need to retain them in the long run, especially the top half of the performing ones. People leaders would have also noted that with baby boomers reaching the retirement junction, it is important for Gen X to pass the baton.

Mentor them to align with the current market scenario and the company's expectations from them. They themselves also need to work on their overall willingness and attitude towards training. They are also required to engage team members and Gen Y in particular.

Gen X also needs to be convinced on the interventions and its return of investment, to ensure effectiveness. Maybe sometimes we can use the funnelling technique of hearing the solution from them. The excess usage of the same is not advisable.

From the survey, it was evident that Gen X can be effectively trained by:

Match #1   Web-based teachings: it is effective, less time consuming, and can be accessed from anywhere, on the move. Some of the evaluation can be quick and online too. When we know as leaders that Gen X is motivated by modern technology, we need to use it as a buy-in from them.

Match #2   Challenging the concepts through a question-based approach can create 'the magic'. That's their style of leadership, so let them follow the same approach as learners too.

Match #3   Brief and easy to read material: learning material with facts, figures, and an easy to read synopsis attracts them. If you send an e-book of 20 pages, it is going to lie in the junk mail section only. So be careful of what you plan. Also, follow ups after trainings are important.

A big learning was when I was working in hotels. We designed an external workshop for leaders of the hotel. It was a three day workshop by Franklin Covey Institute, managing the leaders.

At the beginning of the workshop, I had demanded two important things from the institute. One trainer has to be high end, and all the participants should be leaders. Homework is not advisable. No one would do the same.

I knew the organisation in and out. Incidentally, including me, none of the participants completed their post-training work. It was important, and I realise it today, that the post-training could have been handled better.

Sometimes, you would be unsuccessful, unless there is a buy-in for the same. Enrolling people is very important part of the futuristic language at an organisational level.

Match #4   Offer multimedia learning opportunities: offer distance learning or tie-ups with universities of repute or foreign universities, etc. Tie up for high-end MBAs or PhD to attract them. I am mentioning this because at one stage of my career, I felt the need for it. Send them for foreign training trips. But get them to sign the training agreement as a safe side for the organisation. Retain them in this critical economic slowdown, as they are your prime resource.

Match #5   Ensure access to simple, logically-organised knowledge database.

In two good companies I have been associated with, I have seen two different and easily accessible knowledge base cultures.

Firstly, when I was in Hyatt, I had seen the website having a check list for a leader (department wise, role wise), what he/she needs to do, from pre-opening to opening of the hotel. For example, maybe a 365 days path for a general manager, and a 100 day path for a restaurant manager.

Secondly, I saw a similar thing in a different format at Gyan Mandir of Reliance Infocom. It had basic training module, employee self-service, etc., all available with a simple click; a very high-end employee self-service (ESS).

Match #6   Graphs and designs to be included in presentations, classwork, and assignments.

Match #7   During any learning intervention, the group needs to be handled with regular breaks, as they have a very short span of attention. They will also learn more in an informal, outbound, or all exercise-bound trainings. This can also be clubbed with learnings through games like paint ball, rock climbing, rappelling, etc., ensuring high-end bonding. This would also let you know as a leader a very important thing, which we normally miss, which is, how do they protect the weakest link of the chain or their teams? That would confer a lot of insight into how much stress and planning methodology do they have in them. The fear of failure can also be taken out by these exercises.

Match #8   Use innovative inductions like teambuilding, theatres, especially for IT professionals or engineers. Make them uncomfortable to get the best out of them. You will know their attitude, teamwork, talent, communication, and leadership skills, in a short span of time.

Leaders would second my thoughts when I say that Gen X is making the most significant impact in the workplace as of today. They are empowered, customer-oriented, technology savvy, and not afraid to speak up for change in their workplace.

For them, the theory suits perfectly. Approximately 10 per cent learning takes place in formal training, 20 per cent in material, and IT systems such as books, etc., but the remaining 70 per cent is on the job.

They think of challenging the status-quo; work from morning till noon, take off in the afternoon, and then re-start at 4 pm, and continue till 9 pm.

> I will give you my example. After coming back from office, I love to relax, eat, take a short nap, and then write from 11 pm till 4 am or 5 am. My colleagues feel I am insane. Then how am I able to handle a full day's work pressure? How do I do it day in and out?
>
> Incidentally, I travel every weekend to be with my family which is 1500 km away. These two days are for my family, and not work.
>
> There is no sympathy I wish to gain here. It is just attuning myself and my software and do what I love doing. It is the pleasure in the moment which makes the difference.

Everything is practical as long as you get your work done, and meet and exceed customer expectations and improve productivity. We need to look at a very interesting thing as leaders: 'made-to-order employment relationships'. It is important not to worry about nine to six, till the member is delivering more than 100 on the mutually decided matrix.

Most of the workplaces today are loaded with stress. There was also an interesting fact which came out from leader in my survey. It was that they did not see any noticeable deterioration in workers across generations. The single factor that impacts the level of performance is training.

Gen X needs to mix up the learning opportunities. They need to be mostly self-directed and self-paced, with a purposeful buy-in. Show them the return of investment, and they would understand the impact of it on balance sheet.

High accessibility was shown to the e-learning series of structure lecturers. They required integration of technology and media in learning. Make it easy for them to access the information and industry procedures.

Though I always say age is just a number, and with today's outlook of life, we are living more and healthily. Interesting, I have seen more hyper tension patients in Gen X, than in the next generation of baby boomers. This may be because of our lifestyle. They are sometimes more healthier than us.

Let's look at the elder workforce in our next segment of employees, and compare them with the first two.

> On a lighter note, somebody was telling me that his father in-law needs only one Hajmola (digestive tablet) a day, and he himself needs two diabetics and two hyper tension medicines daily. You can intercept the fitness level of elder generations and their healthy life style.

Key Learnings:

The middle generation needs to believe in the overall mission of its leadership team and organisation. They have a lot of self-pride, ego, or recognition needs. The performance of an organisation mostly depends on these frontline supervisors and managers, as they control and manage teams. It is very important therefore to have this group engaged. They believe in blended cultures, freedom, adaptability, flexibility, and are quite close to the younger lot when it comes to the usage of technology. Measurable and timely booties, distinguishing between performers and non-performers, empowerment, trendy gifts, and clear set of expectations, would motivate them.

CHAPTER 11

'Match the Age': Engaging Baby Boomers*

Key Objectives

- 'Match the age' and define 'baby boomers'.
- 'Matching the age'.
- Expert opinion.
- Misconceptions about baby boomers.
- Entrepreneurial leadership: making it happen, and thinking out of the box.
- 'Match the age' — flexible retirement options.
- 'Match the age' — workforce planning.
- Vision for the future.
- 'Match the age' — attracting mature workers.
- Mature workers — 'match the age' to 'keep them engaged'.

Sometimes, in some specific roles, you need to have a specific actor to confer maturity. We hear movie projects getting delayed, or even shelved, if the actor refuses to do so. Also, as there is no replacement for the talent he has, the director may feel that no one else can do justice to it.

Sometimes, even as a viewer, we come across a character that leaves such an impression, that imagining, someone else essaying that role becomes unfathomable. For example, if I watch Shahenshah, it will always be Amitabh Bachhan. If I think about Godfather, it would always be Marlon Brando. No one can replace them; they are legends.

How do you 'match the age'?

---

*Baby Boomers: Employees of the age group above 46 years

The third and one of the most interesting and experienced workforce we have, are the 'baby boomers'. They are referred in this chapter as the age group of 46 plus.

The increase in birth rate and decrease in death rate is a challenge for entrepreneurial leaders. One good news is that, the level of fitness of this age group of employees has increased. The biggest indicator to what I am saying can be taken from the fact that the Government of India is trying to pass a resolution to move the retirement age further. As people leaders, we are also aware that aging working population, which is one of the largest chunk of workforce in India, is heading towards retirement.

Maybe due to the overall atmosphere and healthy practices, this generation is even fitter than Gen X.

We, as leaders, need to recognise this unique and vital shift, align our teams, and create calculated and state-of-the-art styles of engagement, in order to position them for success.

11.1 'Matching the age' – why do we need this older generation?

Match #1   Customer Engagement.

I think you all would agree that it can be advantageous to present a mature face to your customers. This approach has been successful for financial planning and insurance companies, as older clients appreciate dealing with those who share a similar life experience. That's why I say, even salt and pepper hair work sometimes.

> In my past experience, while doing a customer engagement survey for a consumer durable service and sales team, I realised this point. The customer feels that older employees would share genuine knowledge, and give them real-time solutions, as they are experienced.

Match #2   Work on improving overall competencies.

People leaders would agree that mature workers contribute immensely in suggesting alternative ideas, which supports effective decision making. It also helps in forecasting, which is an important part of budgeting exercises. This generation is very effective due to their overall experience in real-life difficult situations, and has top notch problem-solving skills. If we match it with Gen Y and Gen X, it may create a cocktail of dynamic new ideas, and out-of-the-box approaches. Though, the role of people leaders as facilitators would then become very important.

You would definitely second me when I say that mature workers can significantly impact the performance and productivity of younger workers through coaching and mentoring. It is a catch 22 situation, wherein we know that on-the-job-training is a big attraction for retaining talent; but our resources are very limited. This is where a mature subject matter expert can pitch in. In my terms, I hilariously term it as 'match the catch'.

Entrepreneurial leaders should take these mature workers as a pool of talent, and then with this thought process, match their competencies. The competencies can be all or one of the following:

Match #1   On the job skills/knowledge.
Match #2   Social skills.
Match #3   Leadership skills.

Now use these competencies or skill sets where they fit best at the organisation level. Also, use our overall Asian upbringing, wherein we mostly would love to listen to a mature and experienced team member and leader, rather than a Gen Y. This is in our genes.

The government is trying to redefine retirement, and people leaders should take a leaf out of it, and work towards mutually beneficial relationships.

165

'Match the Age': Engaging Baby Boomers

As we look at a very interesting aspect in India, we find that business schools are mostly understaffed. The quality of people they need is not available.

With no disrespect to anyone, the teaching professionals are bottom-end performers, as most of the top-end MBAs join professional organisations. There are very few academicians who teach out of passion.

If the corporate world and our top executives join hands with academics, we can make a lot of changes.

Some of the leading executives in the professional world have great experiences, and they are extraordinarily well read. Their knowledge is current and practical. Some of them are great people handlers, with best media skills.

Their contribution in academics would surely better the future generation.

11.2 Experts opinion

Like any other Indian male, I am a good cricket commentator, and it is my passion too, so the 'catch' comes from there. To be honest, I hate it if a non-performing cricketer gives expert opinions about techniques, or talks about Sachin Tendulkar, the God of cricket. I feel that an expert's credibility is the most important aspect in today's world.

Interesting statistics show that across the globe, if baby boomers choose to remain in job for two more years, post average retirement, our labour supply would become stable. Indian leaders should work on this, as we need to pass on the baton to Gen Y, and to the one-click generation, preparing them to face the world.

It is easier said than done; Gen X can handle the situation. But in a country like ours, we don't have enough Gen X employees. Engagement rate, which is below 10 per cent currently, is alarming too. We need more aligned, mature individuals, to handle it. If we let the younger generation be handled by 30 odd percentage of disengaged people, then we are in for disaster.

We should explore opportunities of phased or partial retirement and flexible working arrangements, while engaging baby boomers. The approach has to change; it should be engagement till you work, and flexible life-long contributions.

Harvard Business Review in its 'time to retire retirement' confirms that 'while postponing retirement will not solve the looming labour crunch, policies and practices designed to encourage older workers to remain in the workforce should be part of a broader strategy to temper demographic impacts'.

Mature workers or seniors today enjoy good health, active lifestyles, and are becoming tech savvy. They are well-educated, quite experienced, and more than half who turn 58 in India are graduates or technically qualified. Their job satisfaction rates and pride in work are high. They offer advice, experience, maturity, and loyalty.

What else can you expect or demand from your workforce as a leader? I don't need more skills apart from intent. I feel each one of us can train, provided the attitude is right. Do you agree?

11.3 'Match the age' and let's now look at the misconceptions about elder workforce

Match #1 Learnability.

As an entrepreneurial leader, the first myth which was proven wrong is learnability. We always feel that for seniors it is difficult to acquire new skills, especially in terms of technology. Many mature team members are overlooked, depending on the assumptions on willingness.

Match #2 Stickability (in terms of tenure in the organisation).

This is a very interesting part of my research, which suggests that mature workers sustain the highest job tenure overall. Their traditional values of dedication and service translates into loyalty for your company.

Interestingly, I have always looked at innovations in human resources differently. I have stopped measuring exit interviews, and started a different concept called 'stay interviews'.

Stay interviews were conducted in two folds. In the first part, I looked at the oldest employees in the organisation, and asked them why they stayed with us. In the second part, I pulled out employees from the same batch of induction, and noted down their positive experiences.

Together from these two sets of interviews, I realised what further needs to be done to engage employees of every generation. I feel that was a positive change in our approach, from an exit to stay.

Match #3   Manageability (how easy/difficult it is to manage?).

People leaders would sometimes feel that 'match the age' is awkward to manage a diverse workforce. This diversity in workforce provides an excellent opportunity for mutually beneficial relationships. All senior workers want is to work, and if given flexible options, they would be more than happy.

11.4 Entrepreneurial leadership: making it happen by thinking out of the box

If hiring a mature worker would benefit your business, than why not hire them? Talented leaders develop environment and make it attractive. You would agree with me that each generation bring to the table their own set of values, beliefs, and attitudes, towards leaders, colleagues, career paths, and the overall environment. Entrepreneurial leaders need to manage these diverse needs.

Following points may guide you through:

Engage #1   Recognise abilities not the age.

As a people leader, you are responsible towards creating positive vibes at your level. Regardless of age, we may look at some empty positions to be filled by senior workers.

Engage #2   Empathetic towards each age group of employees.

Take time to learn about all four generations, and as a leader, use this information positively.

Engage #3   Style your methodology to be 'one to one'.

Entrepreneurial leaders should move from a 'one-size-fits-all' approach, to individual, and one-to-one approach in engagement.

Engage #4   Be responsible and be flexible.

Being flexible will not only be attractive to baby boomers, but also to other generations. You should be considerate on final deliverables. Rules should be made for the people, and not people for the rule.

The potential benefits of a flexible work arrangement include:

Engage #1   Increased retention.
Engage #2   Reduction in employing budget.
Engage #3   Increased commitment.
Engage #4   Long-term association with the leaders and organisation.

Flexible work options

The most common flexible work arrangements are:

Match #1   Provide employees with some options as to when they start and finish work by using flexible timings. It works fantastic with non-production employees.

Match #2   Working longer days in a shorter work week. Example 48 hours in four days rather than five. I have seen this work well in a 24X7 atmosphere.

Match #3   Part-time schedules may come in various forms.

Match #4   More than one employee or shared resource for the same job.

Match #5   Assignment-based contracts. Leaders need to be careful on the legal implications which are under factories or shops and the Establishment Act of the Government of India.

Match #6   Flexible place of work, where you want to save office space, etc. Includes all forms of off-site work (example: home office, temporary secondments, etc.). Prevalent in project management jobs in IT. It is very important for leaders to be aligned with such resource, and their targets are to be set well in advance with deadlines.

All the above are examples of what I call 'made-to-order' work relationships. I strongly feel that this would be the road ahead for human resource and leaders in the next decade or so, and there would be lot of innovations on the same.

Engage #5   Facilitate – mentoring and sharing of knowledge.

It is easier said than done; become a facilitator and not a leader. Facilitation of mentoring between generations will improve relations. We need to handhold and pass on the organisational knowledge to young workers, and this would be the best way to do it.

Here are a few things to keep in mind as you map out your flexible work strategy:

Match #1   Your situation is unique. Look at the existing arrangement and see how effective it is. Make alterations accordingly.

Match #2   Evaluate evolution: every business leader should evaluate the ROI; are these flexible arrangements contributing to some matrices?

Match #3   Controlling norms: as a people's leader, you need to develop norms for application of flexible work arrangements. Consider team members' expectations and business goals, and balance them out.

11.5 'Match the age': flexible options for retirement

You start contributing as a people's leader strategically, post 40 years of age in most cases. I feel that a person can contribute even after retirement age in India; if not full time, then in some other way. Do you agree?

> I would be more than happy if someone asks me today, 'how much do I need to work?' and 'how much time do I need to do something I love doing?' Can you as a leader support it? Think for a minute and answer.

Most baby boomers nearing retirement mentioned the need to continue work with reduced responsibilities. They also felt they had good health, and they possessed the expertise needed for the job.

As people leaders with creativity, we need to address the following questions:

Match #1   Projects: as people leaders, we need to look at what work assignments would suit the experience on an individual basis.

Match #2   Roles: are roles existing or are they to be freshly created in an organisation? In current circumstances, it makes business sense if the role already exists, and the skills sets of the team member matches.

Match #3   Made to order hours: what flexible work schedule will work?

11.6 'Match the age': attracting mature workers

To create 'the magic', we need to look at the following in terms of mature workers:

Match #1   Charming talented: mature workers.

Look at how a director and a writer balance the roles of experienced and high-skilled, actors with the high energy of the young talent. Sometimes, character artists are more interesting and are required for the success of the film.

Similarly, a coach of a team sport like hockey, football, or cricket needs to balance skills and experience with youth and exuberance, to ensure success.

As leaders, we need to have good communication skills. The criteria like 'high energy', 'exuberance', and 'youth'; needs to be balanced with 'experience', 'skills', and 'loyalty'.

The usage of fine-line terminology like 'all candidates are welcome' or 'this company values workers of all ages', may help in creating a brand. Some companies like IBM successfully do it for ladies, projecting as an 'equal opportunity employer'.

You may also alternatively look at populating your marketing materials with images of staff of all ages. Post it with interviews of old timers, and why they have been here for so many years. What's their value system?

> Once I had used the oldest employees' interviews in the bottom of the salary slips for engagement purpose in Onida. The interview was one of the most effective engagement tools I had ever designed. The reason was simple. Every employee on the first pay day prints the salary slips. This enables you to reach the maximum employees with this intervention. The oldest associates' interviews had more impact than even a CEOs interview, on the mind-set of co-workers.

Match #2   Finding the right mature worker (resourcing).

If you have decided the roles you would like to fill with experienced team members, it is important to look for the right one.

References and look around.
The best pool of skilled labour is the one you already know. Look around your organisation, your social networks, and references from existing employees, for the right skilled resources. Check on their positive energy and health, and then go ahead.

Associations.
Professional associations and their related publications, alumni links, and senior groups, can be good places to connect with mature workers. For example, you need a logistics head. Maybe a magazine on logistics like Log, would be the best place to search one.

Publications.
There is a growing pool of publications that targets the 46+ demographic. Special interest publications and groups, such as those

focussed on financial management, HR, marketing, gardening, or travel, are other possible sources for connecting with the older workers.

11.7 'Match the age' to 'keep them engaged'

As a leader, if you want your organisation to become an employer of choice for mature workers, you may have to look at out-of-box solutions, if you wish to create 'the magic'. Why I say so? Traditionally, not much has happened in India on this front. Our myths are so highly stacked against it.

Keeping in mind the current demographics in India, the faster we start, the better we would be. We need to take a clue from global trends, and we may find the following very useful when planning the same. Modify it to suit yourself and your organisation.

Engage #1 Communicate, communicate, and again, communicate flexibility, again and again.

People leaders need to introduce the concept of flexibility in the core values of the organisation. Share appreciation for experience, and open the door for discussion. Most senior workers will be delighted with the same.

Baby boomers would love to the continuing success of the business. In these testing times, their respect and thread of positive relations in the market should be hung on too.

Engage #2 Honour their skill-sets and experiences, and employ them as subject matter experts or trainers. You can use their experience and build a best practice bible, for future departmental and organisational leaders.

Smart leaders pay a lot of emphasis on productivity and effectiveness of mature as well as young workers. Ensuring equilibrium is the key to success. Skills of all generations are appreciated by everyone in the organisation. Make them feel proud to be part of the success story. Share their success stories with Gen Y and Gen X in open forums.

Engage #3 Make them champions of change through subject matter experts and buddy system.

It is very important as people leaders to leverage their experience into devising benefits for us at an organisation level. When labelled as master-skilled craftsmen, subject matter experts, or buddy champions, they are sure to pass on the skills and handhold the new generations. In manufacturing or services, they have faced decades of real-life problems, and their more than 30 odd years of experience are always a big plus for any organisation, and equivalent to a master's degree.

Aren't they subject matter experts? Then, why don't you use them to create the differentiator? Why don't we groom them into becoming mentors or trainers? I am sure they will be better mentors than Gen X. They would be able to answer the Gen Y and Gen X technically, most of the time with patience.

11.8 Learn, re-learn, and unlearn (continuous learning)

The overall engagement in an organisation depends on opportunities to learn and grow through career progression, coordination and respect for leadership teams, core values of the organisation, and various other related factors. The growth of safety factors in the last three years is due to the current economic slowdown and job-cuts across the globe.

If organisations want to commit to engagement, they need to work on developing world-class leaders. They need to work on becoming the employers of choice, and tap into all talent pool, and work with diverse workforce, with individual planning.

Even in challenges of the labour storm that India and the rest of business world is facing, we can succeed, provided our intent is right, and the profits would follow automatically.

11.9 'Match the age': where are we?

Consider the following to create 'the magic' by 'matching the age':

Match #1   First of all, leaders need to list down the demographic details of employee base.

Match #2   List down the contests and prospects of the employee base we have.

Match #3   Identify shortages in skills we will face and ascertain when that would happen.

Match #4   List the engagement factors for the team members in the organisation.

Match #5   Attrition and stay interview analysis.

Match #6   Ask for plan post retirement.

Match #7   Identify projects which may be better suited to senior or part-time workers?

Match #8   Build on attraction and retention schemes.

11.10 As a leader, where do we want to go (vision of future)? How will we reach that?

'Match the age' to determine the direction for your business, and how you can ensure you have the right people in place to carry out that vision. Look at your vision for considering all aspects of your business – financial, client, organisational, etc., for the short and long term. How will we measure success? List down the skills. What ethics and characteristics will be essential in our employee base? In the end, pen down the best sources of skilled employees.

In the last three sections, we have looked at the new engagement model: 'match the age' to 'keep them engaged'. I am sure you would have already jotted down points ignited in your thought process, while reading these chapters. Plan your future at the organisational or unit level. You can openly discuss any question or query with me directly.

In the next chapter of the book, we will look in a snap shot, at the one-click generation. The generation comprises of current teenagers colleges and school. We will also look at what can we expect out of them at workplace?

I call this generation in college as Gen G, and one in school as Gen I. These personal terms are created by looking at generation gap between my own son and daughter who are 15 and 10 respectively. For our convenience, I have clubbed them into a one-click generation. I feel from here on, generations would change hands in every five or even three years and not a decade.

Key Learnings

We have referred to Baby Boomers as the age group of 46 and above. The large workforce is heading towards retirement. We are facing challenges of finding ways to pass on the baton to the younger lot. The good news is that, because of the overall lifestyle, this generation is more fit and can be used post retirement in specific projects. They can be easily trained and made responsible to groom other generations. They are also useful when it comes to customer engagement, especially in industries like financial planning or real estate. A customer looks for similar life skills and their customer handling experience becomes critical.

We need to attract them, charm them, engage them, identify specific projects, build innovative retention schemes, and communicate that we are friendly employers.

CHAPTER 12

Match the Age: Engaging the One-Click Generation*

Key Objectives

- 'Matching the age' for the one-click generation.
- Learnings from my 15 year old son.
- Experiences and expectations of the one-click generation.
- Real facts about the next generation.
- Differences between Gen Y and the one-click generation.
- How is 'the magic' created in them?
- How is the next generation, Gen I, different, and how difficult it would be to 'keep them engaged'?

12.1 Key differentiators for the one-click generation

Renaissance philosophers believed that all knowledge is interconnected and derived from interactions. You mostly learn on the job or through master-apprentice relationships, where learning is experiential. Post industrial revolution, mass production in industry lead to the growth in economies, which in turn had direct correlation with education and training. In the twentieth century, the pace of learners changed exponentially.

Technology has changed hands from radio to live chat. If we look at Gen Y and Gen G (12–18 years old) closely, online

---

*One-click generation: Gen G (teenagers) and Gen I (expected next generation) together is referred here as one-click generation

gaming usage differ approximately 55 per cent v/s 80 per cent now; whereas, instant massaging is 65 per cent v/s 75 per cent now. They have equal number of scores on reading and creating blogs, and the only place where Gen Y outscored them was text messaging, which went from approximately 60 per cent to 40 per cent. It in itself is an indication.

It is documented now that across the globe, the IQ scores are improving. This can't be only attributed to education. It can definitely have an impact from some out-of-the-box contributions like social media, gaming, etc.

> If I look at my son who is 15 years old, I am shocked at his knowledge, his concepts in technology, and his ability to interact and work on these gadgets. Kids now are no more restricted to only books. They are venturing into the web world of Google and Wiki, to enhance their knowledge and problem-solving skills.

In last 15 odd years, we have experienced more changes than the last three generations together had. The use of media and the means of interaction have increased. Their multi-tasking nature may be re-wiring their brains.

I feel that learners and their ability has changed, and not the education. They expect promotions every quarter, and want to be general managers in five years, and multi-millionaires in the next decade. While we know we can be fired any moment, the one-click generation wants the environment to adopt them.

The general myth is that, this generation is erratic, spoiled, and unwilling to work. In fact, when I see them possessing twenty-first century skills, I am amazed and happy, for we are bringing up a generation which is much more competent than what we were.

12.2 Some real facts about the one-click generation

Match #1   They believe salaries should be earned.

Match #2   One-click generation cares about organisations.

Match #3   They are better team players.

Match #4   They live in an N-dimensional world.

I have been talking about Gen Y in India becoming one of the youngest workforce continuously in the book. Industry and schools have no choice, but to find ways to channel Gen Y's strengths, and adapt the work environment.

What do we need to change immediately in schools and colleges? Have we academicians thought about it? Currently in India, our learning system is in the state of passive reception. We need to quickly come out of that mode and upgrade our facilitating style, as the one-click generation is all about interaction and engagement. Learning has to be interactive, collaborative, shared, distributed, co-authored, and engaging for these kids.

Gamification of learning will help them to be more interactive. It will improve engagement, build feedback and assessment, and problem-solving skills. Constant action and reaction would help Gen G.

'The magic' can be created by teamwork, leadership, and community involvement. One-click loves to work with others, divide tasks, coordinate efforts, communicate via media, and share goals.

The differentiator can be created by multi-tasking and detail orientation. They love to attend to multiple channels, audio-visual input, spoken/written text, and graphical information displays. They can integrate this information to make decisions. They prioritise incoming data according to goals.

Next generation has a benefit because they are good at social networking, games, virtual presence, collaboration, and collective intelligence. The one-click generation is now experiencing alternate reality games.

The future looks very immersive, social, negotiated, collaborative, virtual, and augmented. You want to empower them, but not give up too much control. Direct them towards the right career path according to their strengths and weaknesses.

12.3 Let's together list down the steps which might create 'the magic'

Engage #1   Start early and mentor them at early ages.

Engage #2   invite your kids into a giving process.

Engage #3   Help them with the resources they need; they want to be informed and feel empowered.

Engage #4   Give them autonomy that builds confidence and allows them to take risks.

Engage #5   Expectations should be cleared and ground rules should be stated right at the beginning.

Engage #6   They learn from experience, so share your experiences with them in all situations. Tell them how you got where you are.

For the one-click generation, it is important to identify mentors in the family and outside like teachers, coaches, and spiritual leaders, who can help and guide your youngsters. Empathy and gratitude should be incorporated in our teaching techniques. Allowances should be given (like a pocket money), but with specific guidelines and expectations. Reward, and tick every saving and quality spend.

Create hands-on learning experiences by offering opportunities. They learn fastest if it's an experience driven by peers, for example, cousins or siblings. If this can be launched, it can create 'the magic'.

In the next section, we would look at engagement as a whole, in the current volatile market. We would list down how to be successful in these times. We all need to be on our toes and go and support each other to achieve the numbers.

Key Learnings

The one-click generation comprises of Gen G (12–18 years old) and Gen I, and this generation would be the next in line. In the Indian scenario, it is very important to understand and nurture these young minds. They differ from Gen Y also, in terms of the usage of gaming, messaging, and downloading ratios. They are far more active in social media and closer to technology.

They believe in self-learning, they care about organisations, and are better team players. They live more in a virtual world. Gamification of learning may improve teamwork, leadership, and community involvement.

What can create magic for them? Mentoring at early ages, giving them responsibilities, inviting them into a giving process, provide resources, give them autonomy, clarifying expectations, and sharing experiential learnings, would help. Incorporation of empathy and gratitude would also be beneficial. They learn faster with peer experience.

CHAPTER 13

'Match the Age' – 'Keep them Engaged' during Uncertain Times

Key Objectives

- Current market volatility and why 'keeping them engaged' is so important.
- Organisation-wide sustained determination.
- 'Keep them engaged' – leader directed efforts.
- 'Keep them engaged' – team members directed efforts.
- Conclusion.

Normally, a producer of a movie has an overall control over the budgets. Some of them have huge budgets, and some don't. In difficult times, expenses are often cut to meet the ends, without compromising on quality. This is also a very important leadership quality, which can be termed as budgeting and controlling. Though it is not a book on finance and financial trends, but as entrepreneurial leaders, we should ensure that we keep a tab on it, especially in the current testing times.

I call this approach simply in my words, Triple S; serve better, produce sufficient, and save smarter. This should be the motto of our lives.

I was with the Oberoi Hotels when

we were hit by terrorists, which it had a direct impact on the business. We had to support operations by going to 'zero budgets'. In those testing times, we came up with Triple S. I feel every professional should have this mantra of success in life. Every penny saved is every penny earned.

The current period of economic uncertainty is providing both, opportunities and challenges to the work environment in organisations around the globe. These have a rippling effect, which forced me to pen down my thoughts on the same.

I am sure many of us have gone through this instability once in our lives. But, most of the young workforce is facing this disruption for the first time in their lives. Currently, many organisations are bleeding, and only the fittest would survive; therefore, people leaders need to gear up for the social piece of management. It is amazing how Darwin's theory 'survival of the fittest', always remains in business! Because of an unsure future, change and tentativeness have become permanent, and the decision-taking ability and evaluating risk factors become the most important skills.

India, on the other hand, is also going through a very turbulent political scenario. People don't know whom to trust. This naturally leads to more insecurity in the overall atmosphere. This may be a time of uncertainty, concern, and even fear for those who are not sure what to expect. Though there is lot of hope in the air as I pen down the chapter, but only time would decide which way we go.

As entrepreneurial leaders, we need to answer a few questions. Why do we need to engage during these uncertain periods? Why don't we focus, only on business, as it is the key to surviving? If we agree, then how do we engage during turbulences? What are the steps we can take as people leaders? What can we do? What can an employee do? Will it help the organisation overall?

I have noticed that over a period of time, in this uncertainty, you tend to be more confused. Before we look at how to create an engaging environment, let us consider why engagement during times of turbulence is so important? Let's together explore the possibilities.

There has always been a correlation between performance, productivity, and engagement. We have seen in previous chapters, over 85 per cent of engaged employees are less likely to leave the organisation and produce 20 per cent more than the other team members. In fact, two of the earlier studies on employee engagement conducted by Watson Wyatt found that 'high commitment' organisations (those with loyal and dedicated employees), out-performed low-commitment' organisations by 47 per cent in one study, and 200 per cent in another study.

Most of us would have already got a directive to be on zero budget. I have always maintained that budget is not a deterrent if your intent and planning is right. I expect you all to be with me on this.

Highly engaged employees are linked to higher level of performance and are innovative towards delivering solutions in tough times. We as entrepreneurial leaders need this support, isn't it? When you are in line with the organisation's missions and goals, you are also in line and support of its existence. You know how to work towards making it superior, or a market leader, in terms of competition. The core values of the organisation and leadership teams would need an extraordinary effort from you, and it is only possible if you are mentally and physically present in the job.

Always remember as people managers, especially in front-end jobs, the people are very important, as they are dealing directly with customers. Any dip in their positivity would affect your productivity directly, and may damage your image permanently. It can affect the moment of truth in a negative way. There is a huge difference between service with smile and frown. It is evident on the face.

Customer expectations are also increasing in a 24X7 scenario of service demands. So it is important to have right, motivated, and to top it up, empowered resources, to manage this with a smile. Keeping in mind the feedback by leaders in these testing times, I have come up with some suggestions.

13.1 'Keeping them engaged' in testing times through organisation-wide sustained determination

Entrepreneurial leaders would know that the desire to motivate may have an impact, but real motivation comes from within. Employees are engaged only when they are aligned to the leadership of the organisation and overall organisation values in itself. It is their passion and choice to be part of you. So what's in your hands? You have to create an environment by providing resources to build commitments.

Engage #1 Your primary focus as people leaders should be long and short-term vision and mission

Changing times demand for changing mission of an organisation and your teams. These tough times also bring with them insecurity and uncertainty. It is the time for organisational leaders to communicate extensively; be always transparent, clear, and lead your employees to the right path. It is easier said than done, but it is our responsibility to clarify the new vision of the organisation, and the changes that unfold.

Some of you would debate with me that why to create more confusion? I say, it is important to communicate and be crystal clear in terms of plans, strategies, and the road ahead, with alternations in the current market.

It would enable each of your team members to share their thoughts and ideas. Use funnelling technique with some deliberation, and strengthen the overall organisations. This is a mantra for success.

Engage #2 Entrepreneurial leaders should adjust their outlook depending on the current situation

Times of change bring in lots of uncertainty among all of us. It is here that entrepreneurial leaders have to balance stability, with people drive and management issues. Only honest people leaders would make an impact. Leaders who are careful but are not scared of the change; who can adapt to the situation, and change the prospect and react in adversities very swiftly, are the most successful ones. Communication of course remains the most important factor in building trust. It would be a key differentiator between good and great people leader, and will have positive side effects in the long run.

Each and every team member has to support the leader. I have often seen that a leader gets more support from an engaged team, than from a disengaged one. During this unique transition, people leaders play the role of stabilisers.

Have you observed the ingredients while making a loaf of bread or a bread roll? You have flour, milk, sugar, yeast, etc. You also add a pinch of salt to it. What's the role of salt? It stabilises the flour. Even a pinch sometimes makes a difference to the overall bread. Do not forget to add it whenever you need to stabilise the flour or stop the yeast from over reacting in any baked product. There is also a lesson of leadership in it. What's that? Every player, however small he is, has a role in the team and its success.

It is so nice to see that even in testing times, engaged teams are united with a leader. Approximately 45 per cent of engaged employees have stated that they would support their leaders and organisations, even if the organisation is struggling to succeed.

Engage #3   Dialogue should carry on. Leaders should not close the channel of communication. As I mentioned previously, communication is the key differentiator between a good and great leader, and a good and a great organisation.

In India, 80 per cent of the facts and figures are distorted. In uncertainty, if you try and hide information, rumours will start, and team members will be demotivated.

It is important for people leaders to share correct information and close all channels of miscommunication. They are like your family, and there is nothing to hide. If there is no information, admit it, and share it as and when you have the same. Conduct open-house discussions and keep all your doors and windows open.

> I had started a two-way approach. Number one, I had built an e-mail id called HR.COMMUNICATION to communicate at an organisational level.
>
> Secondly, I built a help desk with a 24 hours turnaround time, and called it HR.HELPDESK. This opened the first channel of all communication.
>
> Once we were done with that, we went a step forward. We designed an innovative concept of the HR head directly communicating with all employees monthly, in an open and direct forum. All issues were noted and closed.
>
> During this process, I travelled fortnightly to every local office, and kept 2–3 hours open for anyone to walk in and speak to me. We took note of all the problems and tried closing them. For outstations, I used videoconferencing and Skype, to reduce my travel costs.
>
> Leaders importantly should close all the issues, and communicate reason for non-closure within the turnaround time. It reassures team members, that as a leader, you are there with them in their testing times. They will surely reciprocate positively.
>
> This has helped me thrice in my career, at different levels, and at different stages.

Building trust takes a lot of time, and breaking it takes a second. If this trust is broken, engaging employees become significantly more difficult. We have spoken about trust previously, and I am its strong preacher. The power of trust is very potent.

Engage #4   Leaders should set the ball rolling (set expectations).

Stress and distraction increases among team members, and it can make organisations less productive. Leaders need to keep their overall organisational focus on high levels of production and thought leadership. People leaders should not allow performance standards to drop. Showing sensitivity in no ways should be taken in with a pinch of salt and reduced expectations. We are onstage, and the show must go on. In the end, it's the balance sheet that counts.

You are the relationship or the link between your people and the management. You must ensure that people are calm, active, and productive, which reduces fear and stress. An idle mind is a devil's workshop. Don't give them the opportunity to gossip and spread negativity.

Engage #5   People leaders should recognise the effect of change, and help team members fight it out.

Let us all agree that change is demanding, and it has impact equally on team members and people managers. As a senior leadership team, you are spending hours on creating plans, goals, and budgets. We should then not fail to address the overall impact it has on our employees.

Good people leaders would take this as an opportunity and engage with people more. They would plan it for them, understand them, and make them understand the relationship between organisational and individual goals. It helps in the long run if your workforce is enrolled, and not hostile to change.

Engage #6   Take continuous feedback and follow it up with open discussions.

Entrepreneurial leaders in turbulent times make two mistakes. First, they take all empowerment back from people leaders, and stop all interactions and communication.

Let me share my experience. Once I was working with a CEO who had no time for human resources during the office hours. I tried, but nothing happened. What I finally did was different.

I started waiting for him till 730 pm, and started accompanying him in his car till the metro station. Trust me, it was productive. This became a differentiator as a human resource head. 15 minutes spent were important and made a huge difference. Daily we started discussing the organizational impacts and changes, which we could implement week on week.

Hard times test the mental ability in you as a leader. Be sure to open multiple communication channels to spread information (i.e., in personal meetings, organisation-wide addresses, e-mails, voicemails, newsletters, etc.).

If promised, provide additional information. If you didn't have the answer to a question, find it and provide the answer. Don't mislead the employees.

When coal is hard-pressed, it turns into diamond. Remember Spiderman's famous quote? 'In tough times, you need to take tough decisions'.

Senior leadership should provide people leaders with transparent and clear information, so that they can be 'change reactors'. Their credibility is yours too. Don't disengage them, as they will take the brunt of it from their team members. Don't allow them to get lost in the middle. Most employees have a higher level of trust in their managers, than in the organisation's leadership as a whole.

13.2 Leader-directed efforts to 'keep them engaged'

Entrepreneurial leaders make and implement the engagement plans. They need to focus on the following things:

Engage #1   Vision and mission: alignment, communication, and
        re-alignment.

As discussed previously in the book, organisations need to clearly set
the vision and mission statements in testing times. It is vital that each
and every entrepreneurial leader considers how their team members
individually would contribute to the same. Engagement should be
individual, so that the overall vision is aligned, and the role of the
individual team member is specified. Make each of them feel aligned
to the big picture. If they understand their pivotal role in the overall
scheme of things; in their department, and in their team, their sense
of engagement will soar up.

The economic slowdown is an opportunity for every people's
leader to explain to the team members how vital their roles are in the
department. An exciting picture has to be created, with each member's
role separately mentioned.

Engage #2   Restore faith: be on the shop floor, be present with
        them, and show solidarity.

The leader is nothing without his followers. Employees want a
leader who know them (personally and professionally), who is willing
to listen to them, and who is caring enough to take time to address
their individual concerns.

Use the principles of LIST:
L: Listen.
I: Isolate the core issues.
S: Solve their problems or suggest alternatives.
T: Very important, close the loop and take feedback. This is where
most of the Indian leadership fails. Follow-ups and feedbacks are of
utmost importance.

This is a critical time to walk around the office, make extra phone calls to off-site employees, and keep them updated on emails, and various other means.

Employees who feel connected to their people leaders are more likely to be with you, feel engaged, and be more effective, at an organisational level. Be sure to schedule time for keeping employees connected with each other.

> This is a great time to share best practices. We have done it many times at an organisational level. Group companies do so many good things, which others do not need to reinvent; just go with the flow and implement them, and save time and energy on innovation.

Engage #3   Communicate, communicate, and keep communicating as a people's leader...

Excited and engaged employees are better for entrepreneurial leaders. This communication would be a key differentiator and a winner for you in the long run. This can make/break your trust.

Engage #4   Empower.

It has been proven that leaders use more empowerment matrices than team members, even if they are empowered. They believe in contributing to the big picture.

Plan for ways to continue being productive in the future, and help the organisation. As a whole, find ways to improve effectiveness and efficiency – two things every organisation needs to focus on to stay competitive. Also, openly appreciate every revenue earned or penny saved.

> Place an appreciation tree in the cafeteria, only the bark, and let the employees appreciate each other on available leaves. The tree would soon be filled up with appreciative leaves. Look up for innovative solutions.

Live Appreciation Tree

13.4 'Team members'-directed efforts to 'keep them engaged'

As a team member, you may rather not know of everything; instead of struggling on your own, consider these approaches to raise your own level of engagement.

Engage #1. Under no circumstances un-align with your leader.

It is very easy to become disconnected with your leader. We all have gone through this phase. It is this time precisely when you need to find ways to support your leader. Have meaningful interactions, and not become insincere.

If you are perceived as one of the patrons, then you are in danger. Have valuable discussions on current projects, activities, and ideas. Share concerns openly with your leader.

Your entrepreneurial leader cannot help you work through your concerns if he/she does not know what concerns you have. Share alternatives and offer suggestions. Trust your leader. Schedule follow-ups.

Engage #2   Business and end results should always be the focus.

Discuss how to reach point A to B, but with an appropriate speed. On a regular basis, conduct project briefings with your people leader. Share your vision for the project/work, progress to date, planned next steps, and any challenges you may be facing. Identify alternative approaches, and assure your leader that you can make your work on the project valuable. This would showcase your value now, and for the future.

Sometimes, every penny saved is equal to every penny earned. We need to achieve our numbers and ensure that the balance sheet is positive. This is a chance to showcase your talent and treat it as a challenge, and deliver positively. It is also a learning opportunity, as these times would not remain forever. Every cycle changes, and we are hopeful towards a brighter future.

Leaders will be looking for positive employees who can help them smoothen out the bumps, which occur in dealing with the current environment.

Have you seen a hotel, call centre, airlines, airport, or a circus? What's common among them? It is important for them to be onstage. The show must go on. This is the statement of the general manager of the Taj Hotel, who lost his family in the terrorist attack, and still worked day and night to ensure that the guests were safe. What do you do to such a man? Even a salute is less.

The business must go on, and we still need to run organisations profitably, and keep our key resources happy and satisfied.

Key learnings

In these testing times, approach of serving better, and saving smarter may work very well. Entrepreneurial leaders need to provide both opportunities and challenges for team members. Decision-making ability and engaging teams would be the key to success in the long run. We need to overcome uncertainties in the future and tentativeness, and be adaptable to change.

Organisation-wide efforts on vision alignment, outlook alignment, have become critical people leadership skills. It is important to be with the team, recognise their efforts, show them the path, help them find the way out, and communicate effectively. Studies prove that 85 per cent of engaged employees are less likely to leave the organisation and may produce up to 20 per cent more than the disengaged ones. This can be achieved through continuous and timely feedback, empowerment, and restoring of faith in the current and the bright future ahead.

CHAPTER 14

Concluding Thoughts and the Road Ahead for the Author

The lifestyles and attitude of people are changing with modernisation. Policies and initiatives sometimes don't take into account the quirky approach of this current generation of employees.

People leaders should also realise that Gen Y employees will still be looking for flexibility, responsibility, and the effective use of technology, when they are forty-five years old.

I believe that a leader who allows the flexibility to adapt to the needs of employees in different age groups is more effective at motivating and retaining employees than being rigid.

As the boomers begin to retire and shift the demographics of a company's workforce (In the next 8–10 years, India will have one of the highest population of the Gen Y workforce), consideration should be given to whether the current scheme of things needs to shift as well.

Entrepreneurial leaders should be in the position to challenge the status-quo. If they don't, then engaging teams would be difficult. The current statistics are so disturbing that we need to look at it differently and urgently.

> There is also another very simple solution if you want to take a short cut. Build a view blocker/breaker. We Indians are experts in it. During Commonwealth Games, I came across this term. Did you get the meaning? Yes, it meant building a temporary framework to ensure that the view is blocked. Just keep on ignoring it. The choice to change the status-quo or remain in the view blocker mode is with the respective leaders. I am just instrumental in showing you the beginning of the voyage.

'Keep them engaged' – Developing a culture

Levels of engagement are likely be ineffective, unless several factors are present in the organisation. Some of the major ones, which were discussed in depth, are listed below:

Engage #1   Good quality line management and good manufacturing practices are implemented.

Engage #2   Two-way communication.

Engage #3   Teamwork.

Engage #4   Single-mindedness on learning and development.

Engage #5   Intent towards employee welfare.

Engage #6   Clear strategies and practices.

Engage #7   The core values of the organisation and its leadership team.

Employees are equally responsible, as entrepreneurial leaders are for contributing to an engaging workplace. Organisations must build an open-door policy and culture, where people are not afraid to give feedback upwards. It is very easy to say that we have an open-door policy, but it is very difficult to follow it in real life.

Leaders have mentioned that support and training to employees is important. We, as entrepreneurial leaders, must have crystal clear and non-discriminatory policies, to which we are committed. The implementation is equally important. Therefore, development needs of employees must be identified and acted upon as soon as possible.

Future research to 'keep them engaged'

Instead of one to many, the future of engagement lies in individual-based engagement plans. Studies have to be built on a clear link between engagement and organisational performance, and also to assess long-term outcomes and benefits. Much of the research to date has focussed upon short-term gains.

Any future research into engagement should bear in mind the practical usage of engagement. The correlation between the age of the employee, his/her tenure, and engagement, are also major focus of concern, and not studied in depth. Organisations have normally one engagement calendar or plan and they stick to it, though the needs of a diverse workforce are different.

We also need to understand that the demographics of India are very different, with one of the youngest workforce, and hence, the concentration on the development of Gen Y and the future one-click generations is a must for our overall development.

All interventions or activities, should be measurable. The impact and its return of investment is important. If people leaders can showcase the impacts or positive movement of scores, to the leadership teams, it is easier to get support for the future change activities. Your focus as an entrepreneurial leader should be cent percent towards capturing the change.

Thank you and the feet forward

I also would like to take this opportunity to thank each one of you personally for spending your precious time and reading my thoughts. If I am able to ignite some new thoughts in you, I would consider myself lucky.

Once again thank you for being a part of my winning journey. I appreciate it. Each one of you and your feedback would make me work harder. Thank you once again.

List of Figures

About the Author

Dr Deepak Malhotra is a doctorate in management studies with specialisation in human resources; MBA in human resources; and holds a post graduate diploma in personnel management and industrial relations. Deepak has close to 20 years of cross-industry professional exposure in the best of brands and in all distinctive areas of human resource management.

He specialises in creating visible change at an organisational level through building systems, competencies, culture, and commitments. His key differentiator would be top-notch human resources and people management skills. His dynamic insight is due to his chequered experience, which helps him to provide modern day strategic human resources across all levels. He loves to determine and deliver various human resource initiatives which are competency based and linked to specific business objectives.

Deepak has worked in various industries and giant houses. He is currently associated with IL & FS as vice president – human resources. It is his vision to have an impact on the overall entrepreneurial leadership. He also believes that for leaders in an organisation, engagement is the key to retention. In the current economic scenario it impacts the bottom line through productivity.

'Match the age' to 'keep them engaged' is his first book, though he actively writes in different print media. He also speaks in various forums including the top business schools, and actively participates in social media. Dr Malhotra is one of the top human resource influencers in the country on social media.